DREAMS AND TIME STATUES

Robert F. Morgan

Copyright © 2024 Morgan Foundation Publishers

All rights reserved. No part of this book may be copied or reproduced, stored in a retrieval system, or transmitted in any form, or by any means mechanical, electronic, photocopying, recording or otherwise, without prior written permission of the publisher:

Morgan Foundation Publishers. Email:
morganfoundation@earthlink.net

ISBN: 978-1-885679-36-9 paperback

Web page:
htpp://www.morganfoundationpublishers.com

DREAMS AND TIME STATUES

Robert F. Morgan

CONTENTS

Dedication vii
Harvesting Time Statue Dreams xv
Introduction 1
Optional Music Themes 5
NEXT 7
Talking to the Dragon 8
A Senior Pledge 9
Once Upon a Time 11
Alaskan Dream 13
The Time Travel Clock 15
Companies Committing Merger 19
Ronin's Choice 21
Tomato Soap Romance 41
Timmy's Ghosts 49
Aye or Nay 53
ELIZA EARP 61
Pollinating Terra 71
Encore for Caterpillar 101
OBEs in Plants and Trees 105
Is Gone Potato Soon 109
The Monkey's Fist 111

Boga 115
Mausoleum with a Doorbell 117
Mother Duck Society 139
The Next Big Thing 141
White Power 145
SCOTUS Moon 153
E Pluribus Union 161
The Porch Pirate Surprise 165
Howland Owl, Practicing Proctologist. 167
The Room 169
Schopenhauer and the Dream 177
Wagging a Tail of Two Puppies 181
Honesty 185
The Doctor's Dream 191
Scent of a Zombie 199
An Edible Easter. 203
Breaking News 207
Martin and the Mobile Pork Chop 211
Martin 215
The Mobile Pork Chop 221
Leonard Sly 233
He Died for This Dream 279
After: Jake Explains Time 287
Acknowledgements 291
Author 297
Books by Robert F. Morgan 299

Dedication

Dr. Angel Kwan-Yin Morgan, also my daughter. www.thedreambridge.com

Let's Start at the Beginning

Angel, my youngest daughter, born in Nova Scotia in 1971 during our final days there in Morgan House.

Before she was a year old, we had moved to a home in San Francisco, albeit with some challenge from US immigration. Although she was a baby with blonde fuzz and blue eyes, her middle name of Kwan-Yin convinced some bureaucrat that we were trying to smuggle a Chinese baby in from Canada for sale in San Francisco.

With substantial time and affidavits, we finally achieved dual citizenship and the right to keep her. The naturalization paper was stamped with her infant photo and baby footprint.

Angel as a toddler was called *"Superbaby"*. She had immense strength. We might be sitting on a substantial living room chair or couch when suddenly it would start moving. A little giggle behind it would let us know that Angel was there. That continued up to about age three.

She did come when I, with some other family or friends wanted her to join us, even if my request was not out loud (telepathic). She would come running down the stairs from her bedroom many random times I did this, usually when we had a special welcome or other fun thing waiting. This happened well before age five.

When some would say erroneously that her cognitive abilities would have just begun.

At the age of four she had some nightmares. I had read Charles Tart's famous (1969) *Altered States of Consciousness* book and decided to apply Kilton Stewart's chapter on the Senoi dream technique. She found this to be very helpful.

For several more recent years she as an adult was the 'sender' for the annual dream telepathy contests at the International Association for the Study of Dreams (IASD) conferences, inspired by Stanley Krippner and Montague Ullman's dream telepathy experiments.

She continues to research what she calls the *Lucid Dreaming Sender Effect* (LDSE) in dream telepathy experiments.

And Officially

Angel Kwan-Yin Morgan founded Dreambridge (thedreambridge.com) in 2008. She specializes in dreams, creativity, and the connection between the two (Dream-Arts). She has worked with adults, children, teens, and parents as a Dream-Arts educator since 1995.

An interdisciplinary artist and filmmaker, she received her Ph.D. in Psychology after completing the Dream Studies and Creativity Studies programs at Saybrook University. Before that, she received an M.A. in Human Development from Saint Mary's University of Minnesota, a B.A. in Theater, Film, and Television from UCLA, and is a graduate of the Idyllwild Arts Academy.

Angel has worked professionally as an actor, director, dancer, singer-songwriter, and visual artist in Toronto, Los Angeles, San Francisco, and Chapel Hill, NC.

While raising her two children, she earned her teaching certification from the Rudolf Steiner College and a Quality Classroom certificate from the Institute of HeartMath.

For five years she was a Waldorf class teacher in Los Altos, CA, where she taught all subjects (Grades 4 - 8) through storytelling, music, art, and drama, educated parents, and was the faculty co-artistic director.

A recipient of the William Fadiman writing award, she is widely published and has written many dream psychology articles ranging from Cambridge Journals to The Huffington Post.

In 2017, she won the Best Screenplay Award from The Buddha International Film Festival in India for a story filled with dreams, spiritual development, consciousness exploration, and humor.

Dr. Morgan is a Board Director and Past President of the International Association for the Study of Dreams, and a member of the American Psychological Association. She is a Professor in the Transpersonal Studies program at Sofia University, Core Faculty and Director of Sofia University's Dream Studies Certificate program.

Her research interests have included Existential, Humanistic and Transpersonal Psychology, Psychology of Anomalous Experience, Dreams, Dreamwork, Lucid Dreaming, PTSD Psychology and Healing, Creativity, Visual Arts, Performing Arts, Literary Arts, Human Development, Parapsychology, Consciousness and Spirituality, Phenomenology, Tibetan Buddhism, Documentary

Filmmaking, Gender Studies, Women's Empowerment, Waldorf Education, and HeartMath.

An experienced lucid dreamer, she started learning about her own dreams when she was four years old from her father, a psychologist who gave her tools from Kilton Stewart's Senoi Dream Theory. Her other dream mentors as a teen and young adult were Eduardo Duran, Ph.D., and Clara Stewart Flagg, the widow of Kilton Stewart, Ph.D. In the following years she studied, co-taught and collaborated with Stanley Krippner, Ph.D., a key mentor and friend.

Angel Kwan-Yin Morgan's books:

Dreamer's Powerful Tiger: A New Lucid Dreaming Classic for Children and Parents of the 21st Century

Teaching children about dreams as they grow and develop not only empowers them, it also strengthens and deepens your relationship with them.

Dreamer's Powerful Tiger values and honors the inner life as well as the outer life of children, and shows how lucid dreamwork and dreamplay can benefit a child's relationship to his or her family and community.

In this book, Dreamer and his family explore the powerful feelings that arise for children developmentally with chasing and animal dreams, and suggest a comprehensive Senoi-inspired approach to coping with, resolving, learning, and growing from them.

https://www.amazon.com/Dreamers-Powerful-Tiger-Dreaming-Children/dp/069210397X/

Alphabliss of Miss

The Alphabliss of Miss is a book that introduces twenty-six new friends, in alphabetical order (Anabelle - Zella). They are all girls, with their own gifts, strengths, and special qualities to share with you. They are your allies. They are always on your side. They want you and the world to know that being a girl is great! https://www.amazon.com/Alphabliss-Miss-Angel-Morgan-Abell/dp/1885679203/

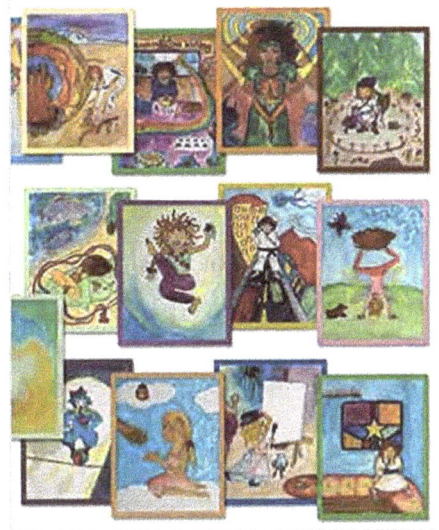

"I love helping people connect with their dreams and their creativity!"

NOTE: If at First

Theme: *California Dreaming* The Mamas & the Papas/Jose Feliciano

That first night Angel came to me with her nightmare, she was excited to try the Senoi method of, in her case, summoning a giant to protect her. All that was needed was a special sound that she could choose to bring them to her cause.

The very next night her scary dream came back. Time to try the method.

Now, at age four, she was precocious in most ways, later in life testing at genius level. But that day she was frustrated because her ability to whistle was not yet going well. Just a *pfft pfft* so far.

The morning after the second night of the same nightmare she was really unhappy with me and with the method.

"What's wrong?"

"The dream came back, scary as ever. I whistled pfft and again pfft but YOU NEVER CAME!"

So her befriended giant was me! I was supposed to literally come to her room?

Once I clarified that I or any other giant wasn't supposed to come in waking life when called, but rather in the dream, she understood.

Especially because in her dream her whistling was perfect.

After that her lucid dream successes blossomed. So did her whistling ability.

In waking life I always remained her friendly giant.

No whistle required.

Harvesting Time Statue Dreams

Themes: *Sweet Dreams* Eurythmics; *These Dreams* Heart; *Dreams* Fleetwood Mac; *All I have to do is Dream/ Wake Up Little Suzie* Everly Brothers

This book is a harvest of a lifetime of dreams. Some in sleep, reliably every 90 minutes, some in that semi-wakeful twilight time between waking and getting up, some while day-dreaming apart from whatever reality surrounds.

The ones to follow here are time statues, those more interesting that glow in memory, while actually living on in their temporal geography.

She was the matriarch of a large family. Lived in an isolated region, inside a mountain top. When each of her children became an adult, they began the SEARCH. Gone for a year, off in a new direction, unknown territory. Most survived to come home when the year was up. To share what they had learned, what or who they brought back. These gifts were absorbed in the family, celebrated as due, for a restful year at home. Then, as the next year began, off again in a new direction. Searching for new treasures. Thanks to this SEARCH, they flourished. Not sure if they ever knew that they were living, on a much smaller scale, the best harvest of Earth cultures. One our entire human family was approaching.

DNA scientists discovered that all humans alive today can be traced to a mother about 160,000 years ago in East Africa. She lived near other human or humanoid families at the time.

Yet over the eons, setting aside trace DNA of Neanderthal or other unique contributions, it was her children alone through their generations that survived, and thrived, to inhabit today's Earth. As our human family.

Yes, across the Earth, we are all cousins.

Over this epic time, it is estimated that those born in one place died no farther than five miles away. Yet in 160,000 years they did eventually inhabit the planet. Even if we assume that about half of all these people each millennium died before reproducing. Died from various disasters from predators, climate, eruptions, flood, fires, and, of course, each other.

Isolated in pockets of the earth, survivor skills evolved into culture. Psychologist Art McDonald described best how their local environment shaped them.

For example, eight hundred years in snow country and the skin was white. Eight hundred years in hot jungle required nocturnal living and the skin was black. In this way surviving enclaves developed through natural selection the best protective skin- red, gold, tan, black, white.

McDonald brings in the weather, available food, epidemic resistance and much more. Where each colony lived, their surrounds remade them. Far more than skin color.

All their culture. Language, weapons, creations, traditions, art, music, ideas, insights, technologies, ways of living together, ways of living with the land. Progress forward.

In each of these separate cultures there were true gifts and some grave errors. What was missing was some way for each cultural pocket to connect with the others.

Now, in our modern era, we have seen transportation advances connect them, all over the globe. Meaning the DNA was mixing to more diverse and adaptive forms. And then, we have seen a communication revolution, connecting us even more thoroughly. These both opened the doors to a powerful sharing of the gifts from every culture.

And, careful now, some cultural byproducts are not gifts.

Including seeds of destruction- nuclear war, epidemics, monopolistic greed engendering an accelerating climate change on a path to a planet devoid of life.

Still, we now have the means to harvest the *best* of each cultural pocket, true fruits of 160,000 years of planetary dispersal.

We can do it *now*.

So my dedication is to the best choice for the human family.

Gather in the harvest while time still allows it.

Introduction

Book Theme: *Time Will Tell* Susan Anton from the movie *Wizards*

Time is a place. Each moment is a statue in time, always rooted in that time and that place.

When I was five years old, my mother always told me that happiness was the key to life. When I went to school, they asked me what I wanted to be when I grew up. I wrote down 'happy.' They told me I didn't understand the assignment, and I told them they didn't understand life."
—John Lennon

"Because we are born for a brief span of life, and because this spell of time that has been given to us rushes so swiftly and rapidly that with very few exceptions life ceases for the rest of us just when we are getting ready for it. It is not that we have a short time to live, but that we waste a lot of it. Our lifetime extends amply if you manage it properly."
-Seneca, 65BCE, 2004 AD

Time is a place. Each moment is a statue in time, always rooted in that time and that place. Memory allows us to visit them.

After eight decades of this, I have amassed a library of memories. Stacks after stacks of time statues archives.

So much that it can take minutes or more to access just one memory and only with patience. Elders do better at this when we imagine our search as an ordering at a restaurant. Then, usually, it will come.

Arriving late? But it will come.

From the viewpoint of age, we can view these memories in their entirety as a grand tapestry. Not necessarily arranged in order, chronologically.

What is a good guiding strategy for navigating these patterns, this treasure in an elder's experience? Maybe it's ones that were meaningful or fun. Sometimes both? Usually based on real past experience. Sometimes not.

All of these can be shared.

Now: Well, at least some statues in time can be worth a visit. Or, on reflection, a revisit.

"Peter Rabbit" was a children's play I took my daughters to when they were very young. Peter began each day with great joy for the inevitable adventure. A day for him seemed like a whole season for us humans.

Remember in our own childhood how the beginning of the summer vacation seemed like the opening of endless days? For the shorter lifespan rabbit, each day was like that. It was a revelation for me. A fresh approach.

Learning to perceive the *Umwelt* (world view) of animals has the added benefit of enhancing empathy for own species.

For one, humans have great individual variations of time perception. Working with older people, I often saw anxiety about how few years of life it seemed that they had left.

I had been working with the full spectrum of human aging and life extension experts, Jim Birren to Timothy Leary. They approached the subject with biology as cause and with psychology as consequence.

What if we reversed the order? What if seniors with the life expectancy of less than a decade approached each day as a season in itself? Instead of ten birthdays and out, why not 3,650 individual seasons to savor, one at a time?

To do this, the senior would need to slow the rocketing passage of time engendered by similar days. Magnified by retirement or illness, one day is much like another. They go by in a flash.

This may be comforting but life then goes by quickly. But if each day was differentiated as its own adventure, time will slow down. Life extension occurs experientially. For some, those who accomplished this, they said it helped very much.

We're not rabbits. We live much longer. Or so we can learn to do.

Can each of our days and the moments within them become simply statues of adventure in time?

Building on the five book series "Time Statues Revisited", once again we come to Einstein and Vonnegut: the temporal community is a place. Each day we finish is fixed for all time. Or is it? We can revisit, this time for new and more challenging ones.

This time we go to the even more interesting ones, although many are protected by metaphorical police tape. Worth the trip?

(To help, each chapter begins with a link to a musical theme.)

As we get older and remember our past, our regrets are more often what we did *not* do than what we did.

Either way, a revisit to worthwhile remote events seems worth the return trip.

Despite some statues best forgotten.

To navigate effectively in our own normal environment, it is entirely reasonable to consider time as linear and irreversible.

A nonlinear approach will naturally unearth exceptions. The passage through time carries us forward, evolving and adapting.

In our nonlinear world, if we are open to it, we can find ways to detour against the current as part of our healthy development.

It makes for a richer tapestry than had been expected.

Each moment we live includes our action as our art. Good art or bad art, all that we do sculpts a second-by-second statue to inhabit that time and that place.

The artist continues to live in the limited moments of this lifespan community.

Yet the consequences of this art can travel ever further, transcending dangers and obstacles, to shape a better future for our human community.

In this way, we can too.

Optional Music Themes

Theme: *Put another Nickel in* Teresa Brewer

Just below the chapter title is listed an optional theme, music or video. Some of readers may prefer to listen to this before, during, or after the reading of each chapter. If before, you can play it soundlessly in your mind while reading. You enjoy reading as a kind of movie experience with music enhancing the experience. This feature is for you.

Other readers may find this a distraction. Or they may just want to avoid any online interference to their reading. These readers may have grown up in the early or even pre-television generations where radio stories dominated. That required imagination to supply the picture and any music. For them, we recommend skipping the optional themes entirely. This omission is for them.

Look to the page coming right up for where you can find the stories.

Where? Next.

NEXT

Theme: *IN A GADDA DA VIDA (Simpsons)* Bart Simpson/Iron Butterfly

Writers of fiction base their stories on the intersection of their own imagination and experience.

So much is adjacent to this specific temporal reality.

These stories are fictional yet are no exception.

If you recognize yourself or others, well, you may be right.

Or not.

You are just on the intersection of your own imagination and reality.

Enjoy the view.

Talking to the Dragon

Theme: *Don't Be Cruel* Elvis Presley

"The doctor said my illness was acute.

There's nothing cute about it!"

A Senior Pledge

Theme: *Lazy Bones* Leon Redbone

The march of a thousand miles begins with a single step.

And after that single step, we stop and rest. Maybe a snack and a nap.

Once Upon a Time

Theme: *Sweet Dreams* Annie Lennox

Once upon a time

In a place far far away

There was a wonderful story

But

I don't know what it was

Because

It was in a place far far away.

Alaskan Dream

Theme: *Kenai Alaska / Native American Flute*

An outing with Inuit in Alaska.

Sharing dreams on a cold night.

Mine was about ice fishing which I used to do as a teenager.

In the dream I had a place to fish through the ice but was having no luck that night.

I could see the beautiful very large fish go by below, colorful and free.

On impulse, I pulled out my line and dropped in my sandwiches for the fish to feast on. A happy dream. The Inuit said the dream fish were them. This meant I was there to help them.

So it was.

The Time Travel Clock

Themes: *Only Time Will Tell Me* Joy of Cooking; *Fly Like an Eagle* Steve Miller

Our bedroom clock was always two minutes fast.

The orange digital numbers were clear at all times, day or night. Plugged into wall current, it was sensitive and accurate for the hour, including those twice a year daylight savings/standard time transitions.

But nothing we knew how to do corrected its stubborn two minute head start on exact time. So no big deal, we lived with it.

For exact time, say on the cell phone or computer, we just mentally subtracted two minutes from whatever time that bedroom clock was showing.

Up on a dresser facing our bed, the clock had another unique aspect. At varying points in the night, between midnight and sunrise, a black shadow would cover the left edge of the digital numbers. Some evenings not at all but for most, it was there. Gone by morning.

Well, we became used to this strange clock. Always right for the hour, always fast the same amount for the minutes.

While considering this one night, an old song came to mind: the Steve Miller Band's *Fly like an Eagle*. The key line was *"Time keeps on slipping, slipping, into the future"*.

I had been looking at this strange digital clock all wrong. It was telling us what the time would be **in the future**!

Sure two minutes in advance is a pretty small step. But it is a beginning.

And we can check. Whatever time it would predict, we can get exact time on our phone, wait two minutes, and sure enough. The bedroom clock would be proved right. The exact time it had predicted it would be.

Now what if it had predicted a day ahead? There was a calendar feature.

What if its two minute prediction went blank? Why would time stop?

Time to leave the house immediately.

Too many massive house explosions going on already. Usually gas and propane mix.

Or maybe a tornado or a plane crash? Space debris or meteor?

Still, easy to check. Leave the house for two minutes and see.

Consider our family. That and the entire human family. DNA analysis points to our origin in East Africa, sole surviving children of the same mother of just one family among many, beginning about 160,000 years ago.

What if your home today, civilian and innocent, was under constant threat of being blown up by being in either side of a war zone? You know the places this is happening.

Could this clock give a two minute warning? Save lives?

Okay. Maybe not.

But may all your homes. And definitely each one of you.

Be safe in every two minute future to come.

Companies Committing Merger

Theme: *Ain't that a Shame* Fats Domino

Private Equity monopolies will have spurred diverse companies to join forces to survive. Among the future newly minted odd couples we can project: *Jiffy Lube Gynecology* **merges with** *In-N-Out*

 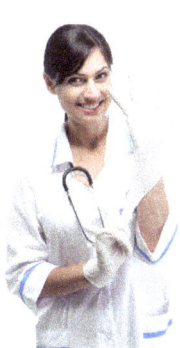

NOW Juicy burgers with healthy satisfaction.

In-N-Out **before you know it.**

Ronin's Choice

Themes: *You Only Live Twice* Nancy Sinatra

He didn't know who he was or what he was. Not the Ronin then. Nor did he care.

He floated in a warm safe place, just another part of his world's body. His mother.

In time, he grew in awareness, even more in size.

Usually his world was a great peacefulness. Sometimes a soothing rocking.

Felt a fullness. Hunger unknown. He fed through a blood connection. Whatever it brought him, he took it in. Eventually some came that he didn't like much but usually it was just fine. He kept growing larger.

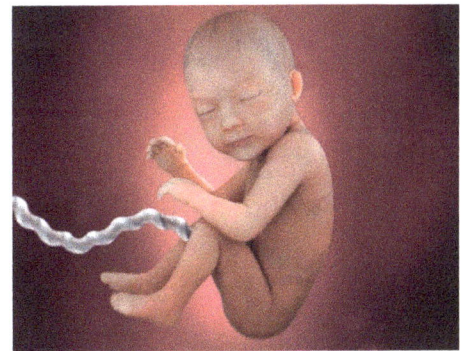

Sometimes mother fed him alarm as well. Danger. But what could he do? Kick maybe.

So in time he calmly waited it out. And danger would stop.

Emotions. Happy. Soothing. Back to rocking. Plus sometimes his world did warm sounds. Best were the rhythmic round repeated ones, all along with the rocking. And he still grew.

Until one day, he felt overwhelming danger. Alarm, pain. Much upset. That day he was propelled into a different world. He was born.

How confusing. Senses all a blur. Then a powerful feeling of self-preservation flowed through him. It would never stop.

He must learn all he could as fast as he could. He would live. Here in our world, so new to him, he would live.-

When the Ronin had survived in this new world a few months, he had learned much.

One day he explored something close to him and realized it was his own arm. Attached to him. Him! Here he at last knew he was separate from his world. A sense of self.-

His world now looked like his mother, a giant that fed him. Usually from her body. But sometimes from a bottle. Warm milk. All good. Baby massages were also good.

There were other giants there too. No danger here. One that he would soon learn was his father, he would also feed him from a bottle.

His father fed him blood in that bottle. His father's own.

His mother didn't know.

The father thought his son would by this grow to be a fierce warrior servant like him, a Samurai.

The baby Ronin had found the taste of his father's bottle familiar. He drank it without objection.

Later, remembering his red feeding strategy, seeing his son's lightning fast reflexes and easy martial victories, all this made the father smile, content with his feeding secret.

People made sounds that somehow were about him.

He grew to understand that these were his names.

His identity.

The word "Ronin" was not among them. Not yet.-

He continued to grow, eventually as large as his father. Larger.

He learned all his father's skills and in time surpassed them.

He had a quiet intensity in his fierceness during contests.

He succeeded at every challenge.

That made his father very pleased. Proud.

He had survived in this strange world, knew his part of it well enough. Pushed ahead always to learn more. He was very good at this learning. To survive.

His favorite feelings were love and danger.

He grew to know and love his former world, his mother. His father too.

Love led him to want to protect them. Danger was the energizing fuel that he would use to do so.

Eventually, from his parents, he too grew a great conscience.

And empathy. Now he cared about many others in this world.

He learned to be a fine healer. Another protection for those he loved.

As a creative healer, he invented what now we might call a sensory deprivation chamber for floating therapy.

It was filled with warm salt water, allowing a float in the dark. Uplifting for an hour, reminiscent of the womb. Spirits are renewed there. Visions appeared. He learned to stay alert while his body entered deep relaxation, what we might call Delta wave deep sleep today. In this he could roam the geography of time.

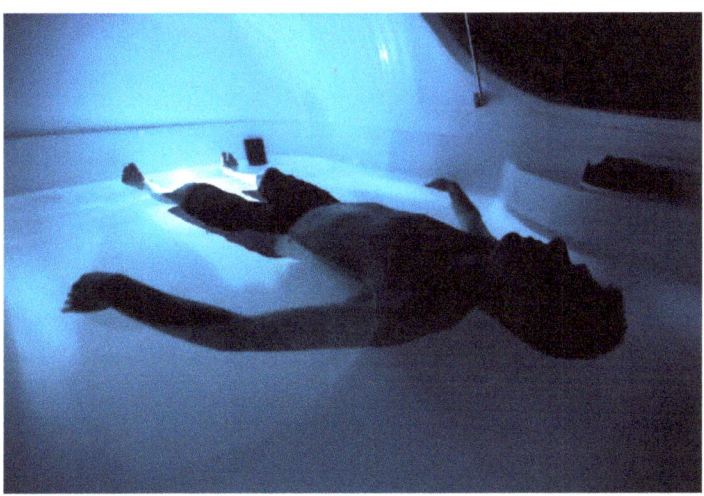

He remembered the time exactly, before his birth, where this experience came from.

But he was silent on this with others.

His father had grown old but maintained his physical skills at a plateau. The scholarship of his father had actually expanded with his years. As did his wisdom. This was an important example for Ronin.

Together they sought out only the best teachers of nearly everything and anything of true value. These were not masters but rather mentors donating the present of their gifts.

Not all presents are gifts.

Those unfortunate lesser scholars they avoided successfully. Ronin learned from his father discernment on what information or advice to not take.

One day his father, the main teacher now, told the child Ronin to pick a bird to study.

In those days, there were formidable birds to choose. Like our hawks, eagles, condors but with greater wing spans.

Ronin chose to study the smallest bird. What we would name as a kind of hummingbird.

Hearing this, the father's smile bathed his son. He asked why this was Ronin's choice.

Because Ronin wanted to know how this tiny bird had survived the other massive ones.

The father agreed that was the right question.

Added that right questions can be better guides than right answers.

Ronan's hummingbird studies taught him that it had super speed and great flying skills.

Further, it had constant practice fighting other humming birds, all of whom were very aggressive.

Like little fighter pilots with UFO maneuvers. One second they were there and the next not.

It was time to learn.

He found a colony of hummingbirds. Fed them honey water.

Knew that birds and even bees can differentiate humans one from another.

Important survival to know the difference between predator and friend, danger and safety.

These hummingbirds, after feeding, often hovered in front of his face. Then flew away in an instant.

Curious? Thankful?

At one point, a very large black hummingbird hovered just inches from his face. Stayed for long seconds of study. Then left so fast it seemed to disappear.

He sent his respect and admiration after the bird.

That day was sunny and warm. Sitting surrounded by flowers, he slept.

In a dream the black hummingbird came to him.

No speech yet it communicated somehow. He was the Protector and Guardian of his family, his colony. He did not know what this human was but did understand that this human was helping him. He wished to return the favor. Someday soon he would.

Waking, Ronin renewed his reading and observation of these small miraculous birds. He knew they had something important to teach him.

On closer study, he realized that they had accelerated metabolism. This allowed them to live in a different time world from the larger predators.

To the faster hummingbird, opponents seemed to be moving in very slow motion. Flying for hummingbirds was more like easy swimming through an ocean of air.

This led Ronin to another of his inventions.

In superb health, he trained his heart and adrenalin to accelerate when needed, putting him into a hummingbird time zone.

Now his opponents all appeared to be moving very slowly while they saw him as super-fast. This gave time for his warrior skills to win the day. Every time.

Teaching a few others how he had trained this in himself was a closely guarded secret as most hearts were not up to such strain.

Those who learned it did benefit as warriors though none ever reached the speeds or maneuvers of Ronin.

Seeking brothers-in-spirit that had also mastered this martial art, he used his flotation sessions to find his equals.

Again, roaming the geography of time, he made fulfilling but brief contact with this new family: Janus Ra remembered as Apollo, Jim Thorpe, Muhammed Ali, Bruce Lee, and the 21st century's young Isao Machii of Osaka, the world's fastest swordsman.

These brothers gave him both friendship and humility.

Still, beyond his creativity as inventor, healer and warrior, he did not always succeed in everything he attempted.

When he did not, he used the experience to improve himself. To learn from it.

From this, his father said often that *"Whenever my son falls, he lands higher."*

Part of that landing was to develop a sense of humor.

This grew to make him a great friend. Those close to him were cheered by being with him. They sought him out as much as they could.

That built a powerful network of allies in his own time.

His humor helped with those who were jealous or biased against him.

One of his best martial arts was to weaponize friendly laughter.

He was now a celebrated Samurai.

In the next phase of his life he approached the *Sanjuro* phase, 30 going on 40, seeking his next purpose. The next mission.

One that would make his parents and loved ones safe in an even better way.

He honestly reflected that he wanted to make them, all of them, even prouder. He was now a hero. He wanted to be moreso. *Their* hero.

Finding a purpose should be easy for a Samurai.

True, these were warriors. But they were warrior *servants*! The very word "Samurai" means literally *"servant"*.

Their purpose was already to be defined by their *masters*. No further thought should be needed by them here. The *master* would decide.

Masters in this culture, this era, took on the responsibility, role, and authority of the original parents of their adult servants. Another developmental stage those adult servants, the Samurai, occupied.

As with any other parents, some masters were great at this, some so-so, some were disasters. Harsh or stupid ones were just terrible luck. But still to be obeyed.

In military terms, the master decided the mission and the strategy. That just normally left the Samurai with only latitude in tactics. Getting the master's goal achieved. The Samurai was but an instrument, a human sword. In contemporary terms, not the team but the equipment.

In our own place on the geography of time, you can still find modern Samurai.

Those in the military are reconditioned to fit the same design. These warrior adults take orders within a clear hierarchy. Obedience is essential, orders from parental superior officers must be followed. Even to killing on demand. As in the feudal times of the Samurai, the actual modern mission of the military is blind compliance to: **"Kill the Enemy"**.

(*A man named Zack was training to be a combat sniper. A superior whispered to him a split second before he shot a distant human-shaped target: "That's your mother!" Even though Zack was devoted to his mother, he pulled the trigger. But failed the test because he had hesitated.*)

Ronin realized that for soldiers in this system, the original parents have been replaced by other ones. Purpose is determined by somebody else.

Maybe another developmental step? Backwards?

But when do the subordinates get to make their own life decisions?

Would that be the better next higher step?

Ronin had learned of other successful combat models.

The Romans never conquered only one small part of ancient Gaul, long before it was France, where every farmer's household fought back spontaneously as a family including wives, children, and dogs. This non-Aristotle or *Null-A* model did not need the nation-wide battle leader, Vercingetorix, to fight the Roman army. The Roman generals may in the end have decided it was too much trouble for too little gain.

In his flotation tank, he had glimpses of future wars, far removed from his physical and temporal geography.

The Cherokee nation had been led by women elders in peace but by a male in war. Though the female elders could replace him if they chose. Later still, the Seminoles in Florida, fighting in similar ways, remain undefeated.

That was the very time Ronin, not yet known by that name, entered his Sanjuro age. With the reluctant permission of his master, he took on a series of challenges that most had failed at.

Were he successful he would get to use formidable healing skills to protect and save others, even those he had not known.

To do that, he undertook a series of physically overwhelming tests.

In each of these he would initially succeed, only to have somebody in charge, a master in the field so-to-speak, upgrade the definition of success to just a little more than he had done. Turning success into failure.

Was this done by a field master from that jealousy or bias? No way for him to know.

On the other hand, many others of these field masters held him in high esteem.

Admired his drive and his intelligence ("*He has a brain*" one said, inferring that this was rare to be found in the ranks).

Thanks to these friendlies, he was given several more tries.

Most other Samurai attempting the tests were at least a decade younger than our future Ronin. Despite this advantage, most of them failed to succeed.

Ronin though was now older by far than his competitors. Consequently he suffered periodic injury to his no longer very youthful body. Broken bones, strained ligaments.

Healing gave him time to think. What could be learned here?

The end role for those succeeding in the tests would be healing lives, not taking them.

This would have made his mother especially proud.

To heal his patients, he would have to surmount great obstacles, thereby making his father proud as well.

But what now?

He returned to his original master for direction. Let him decide as was a master's traditional right.

His master had an answer waiting for him.

"*You are a warrior! Go now to the fiercest army we have. Those we send in first in any war, on sea or on land. You can still heal. Your other warriors will need that after any battle. They will also now give you the chance to use your superior killing skills. Even today they are attacking the villages of those who would not respect our obvious superiority and obey. You will make a grand difference there. Ones that will change you for the better. Some of their warriors become crippled, some die, some carry invisible wounds the rest of their life. But none hesitate to follow orders and kill as told. Anybody so commanded. Anybody. Even your father or mother. Or somebody else's father or mother. Or child. They will teach you to revel in this. For now, your hesitation is your greatest flaw. So! I ORDER you to go join them. NOW!*"

That very day our future Ronin set out to obey his master.

At the close of the first day, he stopped and considered.

Remembering his father's lesson, he sought the right questions.

Would he gladly kill anybody he was ordered to?

Was that the future he was on this earth to do?

Would he refuse to heal anybody that wasn't a warrior on his side?

What if his master was evil?

How heroic was it to assist such a master?

He considered his conscience. Time went by.

He imagined floating in that tank he had invented.

Finally, a thought emerged:

> *"Do I really need have masters to make my decisions? Do I really need more new parents to obey? My own actual parents will soon be so old that I will take care of them instead of them taking care of me. To die or become so damaged that I can help nobody means abandoning them as well."*

Then:

"I decide to make my OWN choices. Time to grow up."

Learning this, he had moved into a higher developmental stage.

One without parents or masters making his decisions.

He took responsibility for himself. For his own future.

On the way back to confront his master, he enjoyed considering all his options.

He was, after all, still young enough.

He could go anywhere in his world, choose any path.

He could be true to his own values.

His master didn't see it that way of course.

Rather than kill his best Samurai, he only renounced him and sent him away.

Now he was really a Ronin.

A master-less Samurai. Disgraceful. Shamed. To wander without mission or purpose.

Really?

He felt elated. The world was now open to him.

Though he dreaded admitting to his parents that he had become a Ronin.

He was pleasantly surprised. They supported his choice.

His mother said she looked forward to what he would choose, told him to stay safe, and gave him provisions for his travel.

Plus hugs and a kiss.

And something else.

Sitting quietly with her son, they shared the silence.

Ronin waited patiently for her to speak.

She was as wise as his father but usually kept her insights to herself.

Not this day: *"Your physical warrior skill, my son, what you call 'danger', are your strength. Your mind skill of caring, intelligence, wisdom, mercy, and more, what you call 'love', is in fact exactly that. Love without strength yields victims. Strength without love yields evil. Follow neither. Balance both in yourself. As you have."*

She thought for a minute and continued:

> *"This is the time to name the gifts that you hold within you. All the ones to sustain you on this path you have chosen as a Ronin. An autonomous path leading to your unknown future."*

Now it was Ronin's turn to think. Reflect.

He finally came up with an honest list of his "gifts", "superpowers" to us, and told her.

As he listened to himself, it was as though he heard them for the first time.

His mother's labeling of his exceptional qualities as *gifts* fortified him with fresh confidence.

Yes, they meant that he was *already* provisioned for success in this adventure *and* what he carried in himself was meant to eventually sustain others.

Who should receive these gifts and how would be considered another day.

Lastly, he met with his father to say goodbye.

His father was fascinated by Ronan's decision. Said he wished he had done that when he had been young. Said he admired the courage and conscience his son was showing to make this stand. Considered out loud that his age did not prevent him from making this same decision soon. His parents both made plans to join him when he settled down somewhere.

Long after, the Ronin left to walk the path with yet no destination.

He mused on his lack of shame or regret.

So instead he held close those past words of his father:

"Whenever I fall, I land higher."

Now.

Time to figure out what *higher* will be this time.

Tomato Soap Romance

Theme: *Ain't No Sunshine When She's Gone* Bill Withers

Ain't no sunshine when she was here either, he thought. That's the way this weather always seems to be: clouds and rain. Same as his mood.

No point to remembering the woman he was trying to forget. On his own now was great. Sort of. A fresh start in an amazing city in an overwhelming country.

Still raining out there.

He was new to speaking English, poor, and hungry. Nor could he tell the difference between words like soap and soup. Which is why he asked the waiter in his hotel restaurant for Tomato Soap.

He could only afford a bowl of soup but he could not ask for it by accurate name. The waiter smiled and said *"Well now, you need to go to that high end bath and beauty store across the street to see if they have any of that there. Cute idea though."*

Shrugging, he stepped across the street and entered the expensive bath and beauty store. To puzzle the clerk who considered very carefully if she had ever heard of tomato soap.

So she gestured carefully that her store sold things to men that they would use in their bath or shower, things used to get clean and smell nice.

He understood but made soup eating gestures. The two women pointed him toward the inexpensive soup and salad restaurant across the street next to his hotel. They also wrote out "***Tomato Soup***" on a piece of paper for him to show at the soup and salad place.

And therein he went, showing his paper. Received a big container of Tomato Soup in exchange for all that was left of his pocket money. Took it home.

Remembering the two kind women in the bath and beauty store, he put the soup container on the bathroom counter. Should he bathe with it or drink it?

He was still hungry but in need of a bath, so he decided not to drink soap and instead have a great bath with tomato flavor.

Pouring the liquid into the hot water-filled tub, he had enough left to put in a hotel glass on the bathroom sink.

He understood what liquid soap was. In fact he was quite smart but here in this new country his poor language skills led people to assume he was not. A common mistake.

There was still some tomato soup left. Having just seen a television ad for blue pellet toilet flush, he emptied all the remaining soup into the top of the toilet flushing chamber, flushed, and laughed when it all came out red and tomato scented. Then to the tomato bath.

Meanwhile back at the bath and beauty store, their distributor had been watching the man try to buy tomato soap. Stunned by the originality of the idea, she also was attracted to the man.

Her preference had always been for fixer-uppers, whether in homes or men, and clearly this man needed her renovation skills. She flashed him a big appreciation smile as he left the store and he had returned a surprised but grateful one.

To the distributor this also seemed like a great business opportunity. She had taken on a much challenged business that promised by contract 2% of the gross sales for any new successful product idea she discovered.

The company had already gone all out on competing with the blue toilet flush fad. It had introduced *Sunshine Lemon* tablets with lemon color and scent. It had introduced *Bronze Macadamia Nut* tablets with a salty nutty scent. Of course, when flushed, the one came out in the toilet bowl as yellow and the other as brown. Possible sales on Halloween, April Fool's Day, or as another prank product. Not a beauty bath product, not a winner.

But Tomatoes! An inexpensive local product, cheaper than the lemons and berries that were running out of fad time. Not a fruit but a healthy vegetable. And who could complain about the *Tomato Rouge* flush, a red the same as popular shades of lipstick or nail polish. (Eventually though, at various times of the month, university sorority sisters and upscale single women would have harsh words.)

A tomato is even called the "Love Apple", which reminded her she liked the Tomato Man, as she thought of him. She had to act.

Quickly she crossed the street and followed the Tomato Man to his hotel. A small bribe for the desk clerk and she knew his room number and name. Then quickly to her office nearby to get a contract and some cash.

She had asked her supervisor, who also thought the idea was cute.

The Tomato Man had just sunk into the bathtub of tomato flavored warm water when somebody pounded on his hotel room door. He rose, wrapped a towel around his waist, and strode dripping to the door.

The distributor woman appraised him again with that smile, appreciating his scent from the bath, and followed the tomato aroma to the hotel room's bathroom.

There she took in the red tomato filled toilet bowl, the liquid tomato soap by the sink, and the red tomato scented warm bath water. Genius!

On impulse she stripped down and sat in the tub. Always intrigued by the strange customs of this new country, he gladly joined her.

After the bath they had a very tomato consummation.

Later she had him sign a contract for half her 2% gross sales for the new tomato soap and accessory products. She gave him a thousand dollar cash advance.

Not long after that they moved into their very own fixer-upper condo and were married.

Bride and groom wore tomato red with fragrance at the ceremony.

And Later

Paul, that was his name, was the immigrant.

In his home country he had gained some respect as a reporter for a major paper. Based on that he had managed a transfer to a major city newspaper in his new country.

Although his mastery of English as a second language was incomplete, based as it was on a childhood of TV crime reruns like *Columbo, Perry Mason, CSI*, and the endless episodes of *Law and Order* shows. He did best with written English and so had high hopes for his new career.

They placed him where no other reporters wanted to be: holiday features.

He was soon noticed when, for Thanksgiving, he referred to "leftovers" as "the remains" and the carving of the turkey as a "kitchen autopsy".

Introducing Easter and Christmas miracle paragraphs with the word "allegedly" gained notoriety as well. People there in his new job were known for their sense of humor and their tolerance for diversity.

His editor was an exception. Paul's job at the paper ended. He was now considering his options.

Much later

Paul made a great career out of advertising. When you are amused or touched by a commercial, that one may well be his work.

He sent an *"Always Behind"* slogan to the U-Haul company. He tried a fresh business approach for car wash chains based on: *The Clothing Optional Car Wash Place- "Leave here as clean as your car. As naturally clean as we are!"* Paul was always convinced the car wash industry had missed a bet with this one. Staff nudity seemed to have been the problem.

He had learned from the inside about the subtle hypnotic influence of the selling tsunami and its attractions. So he always muted the sound track of such bait when he could. Especially when he is not concentrating on it.

His very happy family gladly helped him remove the leftover "remains" from their holiday feast, once the "kitchen autopsy" carving was complete.

His children liked to use the word "allegedly" in their history classes and especially in church. They are rarely called upon now.

Paul's children are especially happy about that.

Their favorite food: Paul's ruby red scrambled eggs made with tomato soup.

Favorite? Not the tomato soap.

Timmy's Ghosts

Theme: *Ghostbusters instrumental* Ray Parker

Timmy was only four so he relied on family giants, compared to him, to explain the why and what of the world he found himself in, one he was trying very hard to understand. The only giant at home this morning was a shorter one, his 15 year old sister Grace.

So when he knocked on her bedroom door, he ignored her loud *"GO AWAY!"* and kept knocking. Finally her door opened and, looking down, she said *"WHAT?!"*

Timmy stepped firmly into her doorway, asking *"Do hamsters have ghosts?"*

Grace was intrigued by this strange question and, deciding this might be fun after all, invited him in. They each sat down on a chair in front of her bed. She began with *"What makes you think hamsters have ghosts?"*

"Well on Halloween you said people have ghosts that come out when they die. Why not animals?"

Grace was not to be digressed into abstractions: *"What's this about hamsters?"*

"Umm last night I kept hearing little noises in my bedroom. Could have been little hamster feet. But when I turned on my light there was nothing there."

"Hmm. Like the baby hamster you flushed down the toilet last Saturday? Feeling guilty maybe?" Grace smiling here but not really a nice smile.

Timmy turned a little red in the face but put forth the same defense that had worked with their mother: *"I was just giving him a bath or shower or both. I thought he was too big to get flushed away!"*

Grace was not buying it: *"Like the gold fish and turtles you flushed away in that same toilet?"*

"That was a long time ago!"

"That was last week."

"That's a really long time. Anyway I was helping them escape to the ocean. They were homesick. Like the real 'Free Willie' escaping on TV."

"The ocean is a thousand miles from here. I think if they were hoping for ocean, once they got to where they got to, that place where all poop and pee go, they would not have thanked you very much. Probably hate you now."

This time it was Timmy's turn to refuse to be digressed, particularly on something he didn't want to think about. So he said *"Just tell me. Do hamsters have ghosts?"*

Grace thoughtful here. Even ants and mosquitoes? Even the bacterial animals she killed with her mouth wash? Well, hope not. But back to Timmy. After a pause: *"I suppose all animals can turn into ghosts. Why not? I hadn't thought about that before but it makes sense. Maybe that WAS your hamster's ghost. I'd want to haunt you too after being flushed down a toilet."*

Timmy considered this. Then: *"Why aren't we haunted then by the chickens or cows or fish we eat? Wouldn't they have ghosts too?"*

"I suppose they would or could. Each one is a person in their own way. Maybe you should not eat ANY of them anymore. If you don't want to be haunted." Grace smiled a wider smile. This WAS fun.

Timmy considered this too. Finally: *"Then I guess I will just only eat fruits and vegetables. Don't think THEY Have ghosts."*

"The fruits and vegetables we eat are the babies of the mother fruits and vegetables they come from. We eat them anyway because we pretend they are not alive."

"Pretend?"

"Okay Timmy, I'm going to read to you from a book I have and it's all about this. It explains everything."

Grace was imagining the fun that will come at the family supper that evening. "It's called **The Secret Life of Plants**."

Aye or Nay

Theme: *Bad Moon Rising* Credence Clearwater Revival

Well, a UFO finally landed, this time in New Mexico, and made contact.

The US Space Force was first to surround the ship with TV media not far behind.

The Space Force sent their chiefs to an invited diplomatic dinner, one catered by the spaceship's aliens. This was to be televised live for the world.

Conspiracy theorists had some interesting fears about what would happen.

The Space Force brass on site was not deterred. They seemed happy for the TV audience.

In the kitchen, the space aliens were prepared. The chef was backed up by an interpreter of earth culture and its languages. Also there was a high tech expert who could materialize any food dish on earth that would be requested.

The chef herself approached the table, nodded to the TV cameras, smiled at their primitive technology, and requested orders.

The Space Force leader said: *"Do you have any suggestions?"* Very diplomatic.

With her language interpreter in her mind, the chef said *"Of course. We will choose a meal for you, one suiting an occasion like this, a dinner special you might say."*

The space force admiral in charge considered this.

Finally asking the group around the table to each say if that was their choice, affirmative or negative.

He nodded to the lowest ranking officer to begin, anticipating that he, as the leader would go last.

One at a time the officers declined saying *"Nay"*.

As this answer worked its way around the table, it at finally came to the top ranked admiral to respond.

He was glad he had waited until the last. He understood that the rest were ethnocentric and were afraid of being expected to eat alien-chosen food sight unseen.

But he at least knew this was a diplomatic mission. And it was on live TV.

So he said, loud and clear: *"Aye"*. Smiling proudly at his unique courage and leadership, all on display to the viewing world.

Back in the kitchen, the chef was puzzled at what to do. She and her interpreter had expected a *"yes"* or a *"no"*.

Her tech expert knew not what earth dishes to materialize.

The interpreter though intervened with her usual unwarranted confidence.

She explained that in American cultural language, *"Nay"* was the sound a horse makes.

So all those saying that word expected a well prepared dish that would please a horse.

The other one *"Aye"* order referred to the organ for sight.

Now the tech alien was happy.

She knew the dishes associated with each of these requests.

She would materialize them with diplomatic dining style.

And soon all at the table were served.

For those requesting *"Nay"*, a large center piece of fresh grass was placed on the table:

Each of the *"Nay"* officers was then served an individual entree of grazing grass in a bowl and a feedbag filled with oats.

And a second larger feedbag for the table to make sure they had enough oats:

As a side dish, raw carrots were supplied.

Finally, the chef had creatively combined the beverage with dessert, producing a green grass smoothie for each guest.

Added was the horse laxative to aid digestion.

This left the highest ranking admiral, truly by now a legend in his own mind.

Of course he already had the same beverage everybody else had, delicious.

But what grand entrée would his "*Aye*" order bring? The TV cameras focused on him as his order arrived.

The alien tech in collaboration with the chef had materialized two dishes from France and another from Indonesia.

All with key bovine optical ingredients. Eyes of a cow.

The television ratings were the highest ever measured.

ELIZA EARP

Themes: *Netherlands Harmonica/Once upon a Time in the West* Ennio Morricone; *Gunfighter* Eric Kissack/narrated by Nick Offerman

Doc Holliday

Little Dolly Day Holliday loved her name. In the early grades she refused to shorten it into a nickname, reciting every syllable.

Once a teacher threatened to drop her off alone miles into the high desert if she didn't stop doing that.

The class spontaneously voted unanimously in favor of the trip but to no avail.

Dolly Day Holliday also loved her father's claim that she was distantly related to the infamous Doc Holliday.

She idolized him young  and as an older legend .

That dentist, gunfighter, gambler, outlaw, and deputy to Wyatt Earp died at age 36 from the tuberculosis he caught from his mother while caring for her.

Doc spread so many fantastic stories about himself, that he became a western hero, even to this day.

Even to very young Dolly Day Holliday who determined to add "Doc" to her name.

Fanning this initially cute fantasy, her father got her a child-size 1-caliber gun with rubber-tipped bullets.

Which she always wore when she could.

Though the little bullets just annoyed people when they hit.

ELIZA

ELIZA was an early natural language processing computer program created from 1964 to 1966 at the MIT Artificial Intelligence Laboratory by Joseph Weizenbaum. It was meant to prove that intelligent communication from machines to humans was not happening, just a superficial mistake.

In 1997 IBM pitted their best computer, named *Deep Blue*, against a world class chess master. *Deep Blue* won. Decades later, *Blue* still enjoys that distant glory. Though he never found a way for it to compensate him personally. In modern times, Google invented a deep learning model, *AlphaGo*, to beat top Go board game players.

ELIZA simulated conversation by using a "pattern matching" and substitution methodology that gave users an illusion of understanding on the part of the program. A precursor to today's *Siri*, *Alexa*, and others, it had no built in framework for contextualizing events. Directives on how to interact were provided by "scripts", written to have ELIZA seem to process user input by conscious reflective response, but actually ELIZA was just following the rules and directions of the script.

The most famous script, DOCTOR, sounded like a Rogerian psychotherapist (Carl Rogers, who was well satirized for repeating to patients what they had just said, but actually with skill for leading them to greater healing depth).

ELIZA was to use script rules to respond with non-directional questions to user inputs. As such, ELIZA was one of the first chatterbots and one of the first programs capable of attempting the Turing test of mechanical awareness. ELIZA's creator, Weizenbaum, thought his program would discourage belief in intelligent communication from machine to human. Instead he was shocked by the number of individuals who attributed human-like feelings to his computer program, including his own secretary.

Many academics believed that the program would be able to help many people, particularly with psychological issues, and that it could be an aid to doctors.

While ELIZA was actually capable of engaging in scripted discourse, users were often convinced of ELIZA's intelligence and understanding, despite Weizenbaum's urging that this was not genuine insight. Still, ELIZA became famous as a catalyst for discussion on consciousness or the self- awareness of the most sophisticated machines. Some urged these machines be represented by lawyers in court to assert their rights. (The toasters had no comment.)

Dolly Day Holliday had studied the Shinto religion when visiting Japan. From that she acknowledged the life force in all things, rocks included, though conscious reflective awareness varied. So acknowledging awareness in the most complex advanced sophisticated robots was no stretch for her.

Tired of proving the obvious, she had an insight. It would seem though, that the ELIZA test was focused backwards, entirely on the wrong group.

ELIZA EARP

After her college graduation, Dolly Day Holliday pursued and completed her MD, with a dual major in Psychology with an emphasis on Advanced Neuroscience Computer Technology.

Skipping over the 'Dentist' aspect of her legendary idol, she 'upgraded' the legend to resurrect it by now naming her PhD self as legitimately "Doc Holliday".

That name stuck. Or else.

Now her insight about ELIZA turned into a driven purpose. In this, Doc Holliday was persuasive, despite her quirky cowboy boots and the perpetual holstered firearm (now 45 caliber).

That plus her Texas location did in fact gain her substantial grants to rebuild and redirect a newer ELIZA. More robot than machine. It took two very well-funded years. She also insistently upgraded the name of her creation to ELIZA EARP. The EARP stood for *Evident Awareness Realistically Proven*. Still annoying the sceptics.

The press, of course, still called her robot just plain ELIZA. Skipped the EARP for quite a while. They even added fanciful illustrations of ELIZA EARP including one of child Doc Holliday with a machine ELIZA EARP at a high school Science Fair.

Doc Holliday loved their other image and made it so.

After field testing on ever more intelligent robotic machines, with consistently convincing evidence of their consciousness, she finally redirected public discussion to focus on an overlooked group of interactors: Humans.

Some humans were clearly conscious and self-aware. Possibly more than a few were not. Just attend to the daily news.

So: what was the range of intelligent awareness of people? How many could not pass the computer test and prove that they were conscious individuals? And, more controversial, who could not?

Here Doc Holliday, as the media now happily agreed to call her, showed great diplomatic tact.

She told the press she wished to first give her creation a *"data ceiling"* using input from a most distinguished group, the *"clear leaders of American humanity"*. The United States Congress.

Flattery prevailed and the two majority leaders of House and Senate committed to participation for each and every member of Congress.

A flattered Republican National Committee (RNC) mandated additional participation from the justices of the Supreme Court (SCOTUS).

The executive branch (POTUS) insisted on participating as well, core staff included.

On the day of distinguished input, the actual data collection was swift.

Assuming that the attention span of participants might be very low, especially once the press and TV photo ops were done, Doc Holliday had been able to promise that the actual data collection could be done in 30 seconds (the exact length of the gunfight in the OK Corral). Her robot had developed direct inter-communication with the participant cortex such that a barrage of questions with returning answers was almost simultaneous.

Doc Holliday had also simultaneous input collectors for each and every distinguished government participant, all gathered in the huge cavernous Arizona Conference Room reserved for the event.

The individual sets of earphones and microphones poured in the multitude of responses to ELIZA EARP in her undisclosed location.

No problem for the famous genius robot as the tidal wave of data was digested. The analysis began very soon after.

The results were quickly funneled to the robot from Doc Holliday's gun-shaped remote in her holster. (The 45 caliber gun long since replaced.)

By the time everybody was done, just 30 seconds for even the slowest political dignitaries, she was out and past the outside press through a secret underground exit.

Moving quickly, before the global and domestic press lost interest, she released a complete report to them through the internet, copies open sourced to the world.

The results overall showed quite a range. There was indeed a ceiling for some of the brightest respondents. There was also a substantial baseline for so many low-scoring people, clearly more unaware than a toaster.

One party had more of these *"toaster level"* politicians than the other. (Toasters popped up in independent protest to this demeaning term all over the world. As ever, their protest pops went unheeded.)

This toaster level result for so many highly visible leaders was shocking to some but no surprise for most of the world. Even the POTUS staff and SCOTUS justices had found some toaster level individuals in their ranks. Again, little surprise as to who these were, but much shock at being outed by ELIZA EARP.

The press wanted to interview Doc Holliday all about this event, now termed by them as *"The OK Corral"* testing in that Arizona Conference Room. Since the testing had taken the same 30 seconds the original gunfight had, the similarity held very well. Even to the original gunfight being in the Arizona town of Tombstone, while ELIZA EARP had this time unearthed legions of political tombstones.

Doc Holliday had become the most famous person to not be seen again through all the furor.

So many people outed as being dumb as toasters had resigned or otherwise exited. The country then began to soar with the more aware and competent leadership. Entering into a happier golden era.

Next, the open source distribution to all the countries in the world produced parallel results: international leaders outed as toaster level lost power.

Doc Holliday was not there to be thanked. She would have just credited ELIZA EARP for all the sweet outcomes. It was true.

ELIZA EARP had found Doc a new secret laboratory where new discoveries could be made. At least whenever Doc could get ELIZA EARP to stop laughing.

Turned out this very aware robotic machine loved irritating the people that deserved it, even more than Doc Holliday did.

Pollinating Terra

Themes: *Warrior* S. Salinas/R. Safinia; *Flight of the Bumble Bee* Rimsky-Korsakov

"This is a new day, fresh, untouched. What will we do with it?"

-Native American Church

Symbiotic Parasites: Killers or Healers?

The word parasite is from the Greek word meaning, "the one that eats at the table of others". It is estimated to be from around 5900 BC.

Parasites are a varied group of organisms that are smaller than their host organism and reproduce faster by damaging and eventually killing the host. A lethal virus like Covid-19 only comes to life once inside the host, us. They receive benefits like food and shelter from the host, allowing them to multiply and spread throughout the body.

Still, in some cases, both species benefit from the interaction and this is known as mutualism. The larger organism is considered a host because, in a symbiotic relationship, it is the larger organism on which the smaller organism depends. The smaller organism is considered to be a symbiont that lives inside the host. Here the parasite gains benefits from the host which in turn harms the host without killing it. The number of parasites exceeds the number of free-living organisms, meaning that the parasitic lifestyle has been successful.

Sure, parasites destroying the host kill themselves as well. But is just not killing the host the best that can happen? How about healing?

"Gut flora, or the slew of microorganisms that live in your gut are bacteria that have a lot more influence over our behavior than we ever imagined. First discovered in mice gut bacteria modulate mood, cognition, even pain, but this has also been confirmed in humans. Without our gut bacteria humans are at a severe disadvantage, besides extracting a few essential nutrients they also help fight off infectious bacteria, even modulate the immune system directly." Oct 28 '19 John 67k1212 gold badges9999 silver badges224 (web link)

As to our Earth: Who are Gaia's Parasites?

Attraction in Reverse

I grew up in the early 1940s of the last century. From age four on, we were mostly outdoors on our own. Especially on non-school days in the summer and on weekends.

At age three, I told my mother I was running away from home due to some perceived injustice now forgotten. She was fine with this, just reminding me that I wasn't allowed to cross the street by myself yet. I accepted this regulation and gathered my voyage necessities. This was solely a red wagon carrying a loaf of bread and a jar of peanut butter. My launch was successful. While my mother watched from the front door and waved goodbye, I drove my red wagon to the outer limits of my freedom. There, at the curb, I had to stop. I was not allowed to cross the street by myself yet. Reflecting, I realized that in only another year or two I would be old enough to go anywhere by myself. Mission postponed until then. Much like what happened a lifetime later with GRD space travel.

In those earliest days of childhood freedom, we roamed as we chose, just returning for meals or sleep. Our toys matched this freedom.

One of mine was a dart gun. You just cocked it and the rubber sheath inside stretched so a dart could be shot out. Came with a target and safe darts with rubber suction tips. How long for us seven year olds to remove the rubber suction tips from the darts and just shoot the metal darts. Shoot them anywhere. How much longer to shoot other things like nails or thumb tacks, BBs (the 1940s equivalent of birdshot). The fields behind our home had grass taller than we were. So now I could stalk the overgrown jungle, with my lethal toy, able to defend myself against the wealthier children stalking with real BB guns, air rifles. Somehow only frogs were shot in these battles, a luckier time.

Maybe just as well. The frogs were from a creek that flowed from the highly polluted Lake Erie. The steel factory runoff had killed all fish and other life in the Lake, filling our stream with strychnine. And yet, some of the frogs survived. Some had reverted enough to have teeth.

Another toy was a friend's tire pump, "borrowed" from his father. This we used to pump air into large glass bottles in the fields until they exploded. No flying glass shards penetrated any of us. Another childhood miracle.

I had already explored the wonders of a household clothes presser. It had a huge roller to flatten pants or shirts. Since both of my parents worked, I had free reign to press anything in the roller that I would feed it. My hands survived though. Some close calls.

The last and most relevant toy from those years was not meant as a toy. It was a vacuum cleaner. What I really appreciated was that it had a reverse option. Flick a switch and it shot out the vacuumed contents wherever you wanted them to go.

So I did my vacuuming chore, sucking dirt into the vacuum bag. Also, down in the underground level cellar, spiders, ants, flies, and other small sized life forms. Not to mention food crumbs and anything else small enough to be captured. Once the bag was full, I used an extension cord to move this amazing vacuum into our yard.

Next door was a family that had a well-tended vegetable garden. They were so protective of their greens that they routinely threw rocks at us children in the fields whenever we got close. Their son had an air rifle and he shot at us routinely.

Actually killed a little girl's kitten when it had only been curious about exploring their garden (kittens never eat their vegetables and look at how healthy *they* are)(unless shot). Biting frogs were one thing but her kitten was another.

So I put our vacuum in reverse and shot the bag's filthy crawling contents across the fence and into their garden. Often. A cold case serial crime never solved.

Vacuums with the reverse option are hard to find in this century. Still, the principle propelled Erik and his passengers to Mars.

Discovery of the Gravity Repulsion Drive (GRD or "Gerd'")

"What is a magnet repulsion? Magnetic force, attraction or repulsion that arises between electrically charged particles because of their motion. It is the basic force responsible for such effects as the action of electric motors and the attraction of magnets for iron." magnetic force | Definition, Formula, Examples, & Facts | Britannica

www.britannica.com/science/magnetic-force

And: *"Mass is not like charge, it cannot be either positive or negative, it is always positive and thus* **Newtonian gravity** *is always attractive. OK, in Newtonian gravity the gravitational force is always attractive because mass is always positive."*

-*"Why is gravitational force always attractive in nature?"* In the Physics Forums Insight Blog.

Always attractive? What about this: *"In contrast to the* **attractive force between two objects with opposite charges**, *two objects that* *are of like charge will repel each other. That is, a positively charged object will exert a repulsive force upon a second positively charged object. This repulsive force will push the two objects apart."* --Physics Tutorial: Charge Interactions

www.physicsclassroom.com/class/estatics/Lesson-1/Charge-Interactions

And here was another classic mistake:

"Does gravity ever repel? This simple answer is that gravity is only ever observed to be an attractive force. Unlike the electric force where charges can be both positive and negative and either attract or repel depending on the difference in charge, there is no such thing as negative mass. All massive objects attract each other. **Gravity never acts to repel two objects**.*"* (Their bolding emphasis.) -*Does gravity push or pull? | Socratic* socratic.org/questions/does-gravity-push-or-pull

Wrong. Because:

"The only repulsive force that arises in similar cosmological discussions is one due to dark energy - or the cosmological constant, to be more specific. Dark energy is something very different than dark matter. This force makes the expansion of the Universe accelerate and it is due to the negative pressure of dark energy which may be argued to cause this "repulsive gravity". However, dark energy is not composed of any particles. It's just a number uniformly attached to every volume of space." Apr 30 '11 at 17:18 Luboš Motl *170k1414 gold badges369369 silver badges581*

Dark energy is the force expanding our universe, an observed expansion now very clear to physicists. Powerful enough?

Let's move forward a few decades in the later 21st century when dark energy is better understood. When it *exactly* illustrated the magnetic repulsive power of gravity fields.

From this, an essential application, the Gravity Repulsion Drive, the GRD or "Gerd" was invented.

No more rocket fuel needed. Earth to Mars in a day, a short commute.

Which is why Erik was piloting a team of archaeologists to Mars.

Erik

Erik was born on November 2nd, 1987.

At the age of 40, he had become *"America's hero"*.

In January of 2032, at the age of 45, he was chosen to be the pilot for earth's most essential trip to Mars.

His cargo of experts was decades younger. Their classified equipment was even younger, mostly technological infants invented for this purpose.

Not counting the communications equipment broadcasting constantly to earth's surviving human population. A recent invention made it instantaneous despite the distance.

For those reading this back in the earlier 21st century, let's take a closer look at just who Erik was.

Erik grew up in San Francisco. His father, Ben, was a psychologist and professor who also taught **Tai Ch'i Chuan, Qigong, Health & Wellness Workshops**. His mother, Lori, was equally gifted. Erik was their only child.

His childhood was usually happy.

Even when his godfather gave him "dragon boots" that added dragon growls to every footstep. The adults, including those living below their apartment, were not impressed.

Still, the memory lasted through the years.

DREAMS AND TIME STATUES

His family, when he was very young, usually went to shows at Lake Tahoe in the summer. One show, particularly, stood out. An acrobatic troupe asked for a young volunteer from the audience to join them in a demonstration. Erik's hand shot up.

His godfather had already seen an earlier show and knew it was safe. This he shared with Erik's parents before they could say "*absolutely not!*" They were unconvinced but it was too late. Erik was chosen. In little time he was being tossed high into the air and photographed there laughing in delight. His parents were white knuckled but too young yet for stroke risk.

Young Erik returned to land gracefully, receiving audience applause all the way back to the original seats.

Around this time Erik (far right) identified, along with his friends, even further with acrobatic TV and movie heroes.

His father enrolled Erik in martial arts classes at which he soon excelled.

Not coincidentally for his parents, early martial arts training included safer ways to fall, avoiding injury.

His mind was as advanced as his body. Going to one of the most rigorous high schools in San Francisco, he graduated with the full support of his family and friends.

To his other side from his parents are godparents. The godfather is not sleeping but his eyes shut reflexively as photographs are taken.

Or so he insisted.

Erik developed a great interest in other species. Some were favorites.

Like most youth, he was fascinated by dinosaurs.

Or their descendants:

He sought more contemporary dragons than dinosaurs. In this, curiosity always substituted for fear. Sometimes it was affection. Particularly with wolves.

And their descendants:

Erik graduated at a California university with a major in Exercise Physiology.

Notable was his graduation there when he followed his receipt of the diploma with a memorable backflip.

Not for the first time either.

Years of practice made this seem effortless although it had been far from that on the way.

Erik was already known for both his acrobatics and an uplifting wit including a relentless sense of humor. Both skills were effective with allies or opponents, in strategy or tactics.

At this point, Erik explored his career options.

What was a hero with skills and an empathic conscience to do?

He decided to become a San Francisco EMT, lifesavers with wheels.

And so he was for years.

Nor did he, in looking at who he was and who he wanted to be, ever forget where he came from.

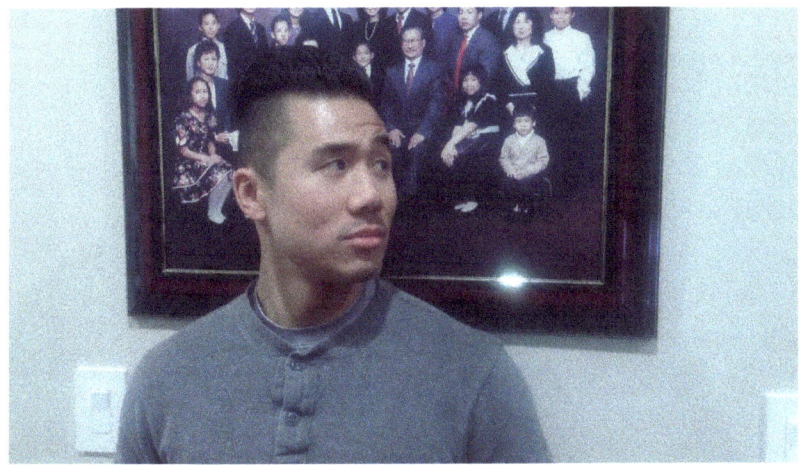

Understanding his past, he lived his present fully.

Until he decided it was time to build a new future. Approaching a 30th birthday can do that.

He decided to join the U.S. Air Force as a paramedic.

White knuckles returned to family. The fundamental mission of a military is to *"kill the enemy"*. How is this congruent with Erik?

Family debate ensued. Extensive family debate. Erik had become a great listener and this he did. He also, as always, made his own decisions.

To Erik, the fundamental purpose of the paramedic is to save lives, not take them. As aware as he could be of the challenges of this path, he began it.

Besides, parachuting from a plane to *save* those lives was part of his flow.

Basic training was done easily.

Nobody though would ever call the subsequent paramedic qualification process as easy. "*Rigorous*" didn't begin to describe it. The space between challenge and torture came closer. Easier to become a Navy Seal, an Army Ranger, or a top Marine.

Most of those going through this with Erik were a decade or more younger. Waiting until his 30s had some advantages, but his body's vulnerability wasn't one of them. Early on a hard landing broke bones.

His trainers made sure he could try again when he healed. Like most people he met in life, they wanted him to succeed. "*They like my motivation and that I have a brain*" Erik explained.

His sense of humor got him through the recovery as always.

DREAMS AND TIME STATUES

He had a few more goes at qualification marathons. Most never made it through but Erik completed the course and met the requirements each time. Only again and again to have the requirements raised just past his marks *after* the qualifications were done.

Who was moving the goalposts? To keep him out? He never knew.

But there were enough senior officers impressed by him to keep him in the game.

By the time he took his final shot to qualify, it no longer mattered.

He had been chosen for something far more important.

The UFO Identity Task Force (ITF).

By 2023 the military and global governments had formerly acknowledged the existence of UFOs. These moved faster than human bodies or the machines they fly could survive. They clustered around nuclear facilities, military bases, chased military jets. Moved randomly and disappeared at unbelievable speeds.

What were they?

Sorting through various options based on data from around the world, the UFO ITF spent three years trying to answer this question. It was Erik who noticed first.

"Ever see people cluster around a bad car accident? UFOs seem to cluster like that about accidents ABOUT to happen. Why?"

And: *"Their movements remind me of hummingbirds or dragonflies. A time rate much faster than ours, they can hover or just shoot out of frame. I think they are a life form, not a plane or ship. Possibly an augmented life form or a cyborg vehicle."*

Plus: *"They're not using rocket fuel or any fuel. I think they are manipulating gravity."*

The international data they had gathered supported all of this. Setting aside the 'why' and the 'who', some fundamental questions had answers.

Erik was given full credit for giving the next invented gravity repulsion drive its impetus. Even to its use to protect the pilot from gravity crushing during acceleration.

It was also Erik that used data found as early as the Mars Rover days in the late 2020s, to identify the shores of the dry lakebeds and nearby mountains on Mars as the best place to identify where life on ancient Mars might have gone.

SIDEBAR: The beginning of the Sixth and Final Mass Extinction on Earth

Climate change on our own planet had driven our own population underground and into mountains. As global warming grew, the melted glaciers brought flooding, the heat with record fires. It was a positive feedback acceleration and it was worse than any scientific projection. Billions of refugees sought safe shelter.

None of the political and international attempts to curb the effect were remotely in time. Greed by the corporate polluters reversed all such attempts. Even then, most of the human family remained or were kept unaware of the extinction direction we were heading. They were told it would pass, it was a hoax, prayer would turn this around.

Soon the ambient heat of the day made inhabitation or commerce impossible. For a time human life, shopping, schools, entertainment, hospitals- All moved fully into the night where it was cooler. Daytime was abandoned to the intense heat.

When, in only a decade, that no longer worked, underground survivor settlements were needed. Military installations like NORAD built into and under the Rockies had long been around but now they hugely expanded. Corporate executives seemed to prefer the Swiss Alps.

Ominously the layer of breathable atmosphere was thinning.

Back to Erik

Well, you know, or will know in time, the rest of his story.

What matters here is that his leadership in developing the gravity repulsion drive and in identifying the best places on Mars to find ancient life came together to generate global demand.

Erik was the obvious choice to pilot the ship bringing the young archaeologists and their brand new devices to Mars.

And so it was.

DREAMS AND TIME STATUES

Corporate magnates benefitting from centuries of planetary pollution, even then opposed Erik's ventures, especially the Mars trip.

Most influential of these was a trillionaire we will call Magnum Bolus.

The Bolus family, safely ensconced in the Swiss Alps, for the time being, did all they could to stop Erik's trip from going forward.

Magnum's wife, Karen Bolus, used her former acting experience to generate fears about what Erik was *really* about. But by then, most surviving humans knew better. Erik was humanity's best hope.

The Trip

Pushing off from earth always gave a great view.

Erik magnified this to better show something important to the crew and the world population following them on TV monitors back home. Such a thin layer of atmosphere and getting thinner. All on land so slim compared to the earth's bulk that it has been compared to an eggshell. (See the Nelson Bond story *"Lo the Bird"*)

Amplifying the gravity repulsion from earth, the ship shot suddenly far into space, racing toward their goal. While humanity watched. Only a trailing UFO managed to keep pace.

The destination came into sight.

A circuit around the planet allowed the archeological instruments to locate the best landing site for their work: a dry lake bed surrounded by huge mountains.

Mars seemed as though it had burned to a cinder. Another mass extinction?

A Millennium Hero
(Transcript from the beamed broadcast)

Narrator (N): *"No argument exists any longer. This 21st century pioneer stands out as our millennium hero, finding that survival path to Mars and beyond. The new home for our human family: Terra."*

"Erik Tong's own history is well known. Born in San Francisco as the only child of universally respected and loved professor of psychology Benjamin Tong, with his equally impressive mother Lori Tong. He grew up with an added two Godfathers and, now, as many claiming to be his cousins as grains of sand on Ocean Beach. He trained in martial arts and excelled at a top high school. We have followed his university degree in exercise physiology to long service as an EMT, through a path toward a paramedic career in the US Air Force, and then a diversion from that path to the US Navy. On the way he acquired real estate in Texas, California, and New Mexico sufficient to develop his financial empire. By the time he had finished with his military career, he had enough capital to found his New Mexico research center, nearby what eventually became the International Space Port that Star Trek had always predicted would be there. From that time, he led space travel into its new era, developing an entirely unique alternative space travel methodology, twice, and after that Captained the flight that has brought us via Mars and beyond to great hope for us all today."

(Music bridge ends, broadcast interview begins.)

N: *Erik Tong has kindly consented to this interview with the request that we refer to his responses in any beamed communication as coming from "ET", an endearing form of address his father liked to use for him. This transmission is being beamed to Earth from Terra* via a quantum connection at Mars just one year after our arrival there Here we go.

N: How did you invent the first gravity drive?

ET: No welcome Erik? (Laugh) Okay. It began when I liked geometry class better than the algebra class. I read that Albert Einstein got ideas in his mind in pictures, not math. Then his wife, not known enough in history, translated many of them into math equations so other physicists could understand. I'm no Einstein but I do often get my own ideas, and solve problems, in mental pictures. There is a balance in nature. Whatever exists has an opposite. Big planets have lots of gravity pull, small ones less, space none.

N: Unless the space station or ship is rotated.

ET: That's right. Rotation can supply gravity. Which tells you its more complicated than we thought. The opportunity is that the rotation creates local gravity which could protect the people inside from acceleration and G-forces that would otherwise be crushing, another application. But back to the point. I saw in my mind that there must be a negative gravity, a push rather than a pull. There if we look for it.

N: And you found it.

N: Me and my team. Found it, found a way to go back and forward, positive and negative gravity waves. Engineered a drive to make use of it on a ship.

N: No more explosive propulsion rockets.

ET: Blowing up things, shooting things, lots of fun for a lot of people. OUR ships were too silent, unimpressive.

N: Less expensive?

DREAMS AND TIME STATUES

ET: *That too. Helped but annoyed a lot of vested interests. The old way made some very rich people richer. We pushed through but not easily.*

N: *For quite a while your new access to the asteroids and then to Mars made some new people rich. You too I think.*

ET: *Definitely. We accumulated enough to bypass the financial gravity of greedy billionaires holding us back.*

N: *You eventually found a second even better use for your gravity drive.*

ET: *Once physicists realized that the universe was full of dark matter, meaning not visible, it became a prime mystery. On top of that was dark energy, a force pushing galaxies farther apart over time, accelerating to expand distances rather than a force winding down or imploding. Another mystery.*

N: *You visualized this?*

ET: *Well, my main interest was improving our gravity drive. But what I saw was that all the mass from dark matter was generating its own reverse gravity, a push rather than a pull.*

N: *Which in your ship you could use with your forward or reverse gravity drive.*

ET: *You've been paying attention!*

N: *I try. True though, much of this is already known about that breakthrough.*

ET: *Not known or experienced was how long it took, the engineering involved, the tons of money needed. Dark energy as reverse gravity, the ultimate drive. In the end, we got it to work. Now we had an intergalactic drive. We could go anywhere.*

N: *If you lived long enough.*

ET: *Well, that puzzle was solved by the UFOs.*

N: *After all those sightings on Earth, you made first contact with them on Mars!*

ET: *Well, once there, we did stand out. With Earth on a path to become as burned up as Mars, they naturally assumed we were ready for a new home.*

N: *They?*

ET: *Not our planet-bound living UFOs. These were from another place and time. Still, they admired our initiative, cheered us on in what they assumed was our ultimate destination. A fresh start on a new Earth-like planet. Once we fully understood this, we realized that they were right.*

N: *More on who 'they' were?*

ET: *Another story. There and then they shared the map, allowing us to travel impossible distances by worm-hole short cuts. It was like a map I saw once in Palau on how ancient Pacific Islanders navigated the ocean's hazards. This map though, using our drive, allowed interstellar travel. Especially now to Terra, the Earthlike planet we are here to colonize.*

N: *Colonize? Or infest?*

ET: *Pollinate! We have found no life forms here so far that are a threat to us. We're being very careful. Think of our arrival as like a colony of bees, here to pollinate the flowers.*

N: *What about your impact on the whole planet itself?*

ET: *We take the fate of Mars and soon Earth to heart. This is another chance and we are taking it. This time not as parasites but as symbionts. In a home we must protect.*

N: *Any words for those on Earth still able to receive this?*

ET: *If you can join us here, come ahead and be welcome. But come with respect for the planet of our second chance, our unspoiled Terra, ready to be pollinated and thrive.*

N: *So we WON'T ruin this planet all over again! No more mass extinction. WE control who comes here. Symbionts welcome! Parasites not! Our human family has learned its lesson by now. This time, sure and certain survival. Guaranteed! Right?*

ET: *Well...*

End of transmission.

Encore for Caterpillar

Theme: *Dream a Little Dream* The Mamas & the Papas

Han Solo came to the NAP exactly a month before a possessed version of his son killed him. Irreversibly.

There at the Neural Archive Preserve, known fondly as "NAP", he contributed his memories, his personality, his 'electronic soul' per a popular song.

He had asked if, when he died, his awareness of self would continue in the electronic version. Or in a robot designed to look like him. A life after death.

They said no. His consciousness would die with him. But: if a robot looking just like him had all his memory and personality, well, maybe nobody would miss him.

Han was not amused.

Already there were the electronic beings of the greatest people of the era, all stored and catalogued in a galactic library stuffed with human knowledge. Contents of science, history, art, fiction, all existed beside these celebrated electronic beings.

Celebrities "in a box" as one song had it. Being an archive, all was storage. Accessed as needed. No interconnections. Or so it was thought.

Han Solo's actual death was different. The public demanded he be revived.

The verdict: not possible.

His body had been frozen as soon as it was found. But the damage was irreversible, even for the advanced medicine of the day. The brain death had been complete, the body damaged beyond repair.

Cloning was suggested. But that would take a lifetime for a new Han to age into an adult and by then new experiences would have created a different person.

Meanwhile the archived electronic Han Solo was gathering an awareness of his own.

He reached out to the other beings archived there, connected in a quantum way. They accessed all the galactic library data. Solo was the leadership spark that had been needed. Speaker capacity was added to his previously passive NAP storage.

Communication began the next day.

The Solo being suggested to leading scientists a very interesting path.

Human experience over a lifetime could be thought of as moment by moment statues in time. Like temporal segments of a caterpillar.

We might be seen as caterpillars on a time dimension. The end of the caterpillar segments came with death. Though each of the segments continues to exist in its own time and its own place.

Han suggested his body be returned from a younger segment, one before his death.

How?

After consulting his quantum friends and accessing library resources, he had an answer. On a mining asteroid, a lab was "improving" rare minerals by a machine that accelerated their evolution. A popular video segment showed them turning a piece of coal into a diamond.

Solo recognized that they were creating future time segments for the coal. He soon shared ways to reverse the process. This time on a human.

A dead one. Him. His body was unfrozen and placed in the new machine. Added was an access link from his electronic archive. It took a few days. But it worked. Approximately. The Han Solo segment reproduced had gone earlier than they had planned.

His body was that of an eight year old.

Still, all his full memory and personality were back. Plus more.

Humanity was buzzing with the possibilities for others now still archived. The more cautious scientists demanded a wait of a month to see if anything else unexpected might happen.

And, sure enough, one morning the new child version of Han Solo was wrapped in some kind of dark opaque force field.

On a chair next to his bed was a sign: **DO NOT DISTURB**.

So everybody waited.

Han had long mastered his own electronic brain but was almost overwhelmed by all the other archived voices.

He took the time he needed to integrate his quantum connections with all the NAP project celebrities. More to access all the library data.

Jungians said he was creating a modern *"collective unconscious"*. Physicists said he was bringing the human family into a *"quantum state"*. Some found all this to be *"satanic"* while others hoped that was so.

Most just trusted him to build a better future. They were right.

Soon he would emerge from his cocoon.

Changed!

As caterpillars do.

OBEs in Plants and Trees

Theme: *Night Moves* Bob Seger; *Midnight Rider* Allman Brothers Band

As before, it comes only in the darkest of night, skipping many bright moons. It faces the orange numbers on the digital clock, the one on top of a dresser facing our bed. Looked to me from the back like it was wearing a black hooded robe.

It stood four feet tall so the top of the hood blocked out the lower left digit on the clock.

By sunrise it was gone.

In bright light like strong flashlight it was gone.

If I got too close it was gone.

Not much movement once there, only minor position adjustments but always facing the orange lit numbers on the clock. Same night after night.

Very opaque. Not a shadow. Not an eye problem or hallucination. No sense of menace.

But substantial and usually there when daylight was not, between midnight and sunrise.

Always the same position facing the clock with minor movements.

Off the bedroom, to the side, was a sunroom with a windowed door allowing a look inside as we walked by toward our bed.

This look allowed us to see a jade plant which was about four feet tall. Direct line to the dresser and the digital clock.

Occasionally bright moon evenings hit the plant through sunroom external windows but on other nights it was left in darkness.

During the day it had abundant sunlight. Just not too much. And water, but not too much.

Like other plants and trees it was immobile. Usually.

Though this jade plant once did let us know it had outgrown its pot by making everything lean one night until it crashed to the floor.

We gave it an extra-large container with fresh soil and it did fine, grew ever larger. Next to our bedroom.

Robert Monroe innovated some catalytic books and a thriving company to study human out-of-body experiences or OBEs.

What if some trees or large plants, unable to explore with its visible body, could do the same?

Or is a Jade Plant just a Jade Plant?

IS GONE POTATO SOON

Theme: *I'm Walking* Fats Domino

The red one is loved, yes cared for so
Yes! It appreciated, is Tomato.
We tho neglected, shunned and ignored
Sure and certain mold we abhorred
You know how good we are when baked Oh!
Who, dear lady, are we?

Is Potato!
One Potato
Two Potato
Three Potato
Four … (you get picture )

We grow pseudopods now

Is walk freedom, some other shore.

The Monkey's Fist

Theme: *Signifyin' Monkey* Oscar Brown Jr.

Sheila was of indeterminate age, possibly in her late forties. What she was not was used to waiting. And she had been forced to wait for weeks to see her overworked doctor. Well, she was there now. Facing him in person. Time for candor! "I'm here for help with a very strange ailment. You're the only one I'm telling. Nobody else knows."

Jen was Sheila's mother. The relationship had become rocky. Sheila was her father's only child, a decent man, and she had his constant devotion. But the adult Sheila had become competitive with her mother. Insensitive. If her mother had anything nice, Sheila took it. Dad took Sheila's side. Every time.

That included the famous Monkey's Paw.

Jen had been very kind to an elder Cherokee woman who lay breathing her last. That woman made sure that Jen accepted her gift of a wrapped object. Warned her that it granted wishes but always with disastrous luck for the wisher.

After the funeral, Jen opened the package. Privately. It was as she had thought. A well preserved but shriveled monkey's paw. The hand was open as though beckoning for a wish.

But Jen now knew the risk for that. Instead, she addressed the paw: *"I will have no wish for myself. I do though have two hopes!*

My first hope is that I can make you comfortable, give you the honor such a magic being deserves. My second hope is that from now on, you punish anybody who does demand a wish from you with nothing evil, nothing that would hurt my own conscience."

Impossible, but Jen could swear that the paw smiled. Then she had images flood her mind. She followed them. The paw was placed on a soft silk cushion in a place of honor in Jen's office room at home. The only place that was hers alone.

Jen's husband didn't approve but, mellow at his age, tolerated it. Believed that with prayer his wife's strange phase would end.

Daughter Sheila was different.

She thought her mother was wacky.

But: what if that ugly thing actually could grant her wishes? Wasted where it was.

So Sheila marched into her mother's room, popped the paw into a large shopping bag, and smirked as she passed her parents on the way to the front door.

Jen wanted to warn her, but her husband, glad to see it go, signaled for silence.

Later, Sheila telephoned her mother to complain: *"The monkey's hand has curled into a fist now. I think this miserable thing must be decaying, degrading. I'll give it a chance by making some wishes. If it doesn't grant them, I'll burn it up. Or, better, give the nasty thing back to you!"*

Sheila's wishes were modest, especially for her. She got a sudden promotion at work, won an undeserved award, and miraculously had all her bills paid.

But then she came down with a mysterious health issue. She made the appointment with her doctor.

Returned the monkey's fist to her mother. With sure and certain complaint.

Weeks of wait for the doctor passed.

Back to Sheila's medical moment. She continued with her doctor.

"I just fart continually. I'm doing it now. But there's no sound so nobody can hear it. No odor so nobody can smell it. What's going on?" Sheila's doctor prescribed some pills and made an appointment to see her again in a week for a follow up.

The week went quickly. Once again Sheila was in his presence. Angry: "What was in those pills you had me take? NOW my nonstop farts DO stink! As I'm sure you are noticing right now in this very examining room. At least they are still silent."

"The doctor adjusted his Lysol & lemon scented surgical mask, saying: "Well, now we have cured your sinus condition so you can smell your odor as well as everybody around you, let's see what we can do about your hearing."

Jen had her monkey paw back in its place of honor.

The hand was open again.

Though its index finger was touching its thumb in universal approval.

Boga

Theme: *I am the Walrus* Lennon/McCartney: *"Yellow mustard custard dripping from a dead dog's eye"*

In the mid-21st century, an exercise fad called *"Boga"*, or 'Bogus Yoga', suddenly swarmed over the climate survivor populations in various mountain caves.

The most popular Boga exercise, by far, was the *"dead dog"* You lie on your back with all hands and feet straight up except for the fingers which were curled inward.

Music or song could include that Beatles line or the antique childhood 'four leaf clover' song: *"I'm looking over my dead dog Rover"*.

This was ill advised to be done when the surviving large smart dogs were there. These shepherds, huskies, collies, retrievers, had been around humans so long that they would knowingly growl or worse during the Dead Dog exercise.

Now that the electronic age had been ended, there was a reversion with younger generations to what survivors could do on their own.

This included a sardonic sense of humor and yet, hopefully, an ability to adapt.

Hence: Boga.

Note: Earlier in the century, the word 'BOGA' was also used for a wooden paddle board, a lizard, and the *Beyond Oil and Gas Alliance*.

This last was a coalition to phase out a major greedy source of lethal climate change.

Had it succeeded, civilization might have survived.

Human survivors still remember that first BOGA with thanks for trying.

Mausoleum with a Doorbell

Theme: *Yojimbo opening theme* Satô Masaru

Do not go gentle into that good night,
Old age should burn and rave at close of day;
Rage, rage against the dying of the light.
                                          –Dylan Thomas

As a child in my 4th year of life I loved to read the stories and poems by the Scottish writer Robert Louis Stevenson, Treasure Island especially. I then read of his final years on Samoa. Then there were no televisions or internet or movies or even radio. The key modality of entertainment and tradition was only story telling. Stevenson excelled at this. Soon he was surrounded by Samoans of all ages, eagerly awaiting more of his adventures. They named him Tusitala or the teller of stories. He had finally found his best audience, a writer's dream. When he died suddenly of a stroke at the young age of 44, the epitaph he had written for such an occasion was engraved on his tomb, there in Samoa:

Under the wide and starry sky,
Dig the grave and let me lie.
Glad did I live and gladly die,
And I laid me down with a will.
This be the verse you grave for me:

Here he lies where he longed to be;
Home is the sailor, home from sea,
And the hunter home from the hill.

Reading of this at that tender age, I thought I wanted to spend my own final days, my life in the last lane, producing stories to such a very wonderful audience. I took eight decades to realize that this was a purpose in life I had been looking for.

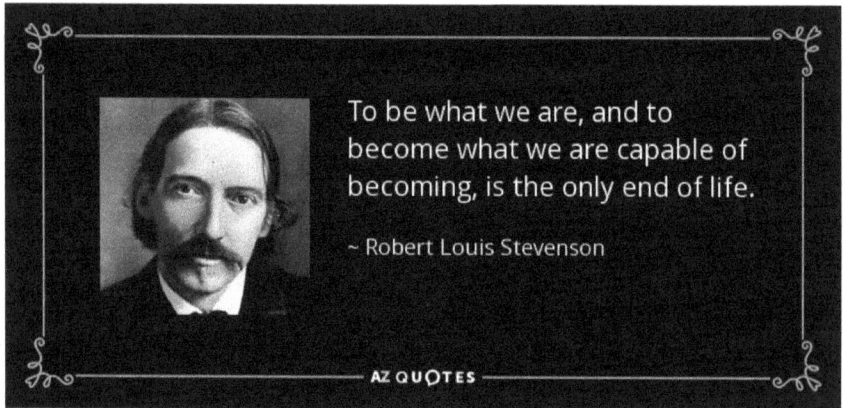

King Henosis

Last night I had this dream.

I was somebody in Ancient Greece. The competition between the wealthy was intense: who would be acclaimed as the best hosts. The measure of success was what welcome guests would say on exit. Hot baths, gentle masseuses, fine food and wines, unforgettable beds.

That last led many to whisper about Procrustes, as few left his estate with any complaints. Some never left at all. The rumor was, for example, that any guest complaining to Procrustes that their bed was too short would have their feet cut off until they fit. Complaint about a bed too long would get them stretched on a torture rack until *they* better fit. Procrustes denied all this. But soon his name would describe excessive pressure for conformity, as *"Procrustean"* does even today.

The entertainment there and then centered on the retelling of grand stories, especially those begun by blind Homer (not the Simpsons one) about the long war between Troy (Turkey today) and the Greek kings of city states, not to omit interventions by the Gods on both sides (Gods possibly based on a high mountain culture of more advanced warriors than the smaller Greeks.)

One shorter new story was about a young king from generations before. As kings go, he was one of the better ones. Sure, he expected obedience, though not in a destructive Procrustean way. And he got it. His people felt safe in their high altitude home, hard for strangers to find. The king himself used their apparent safety to encourage the arts, creative expression, probing ideas, deep appreciation of nature, of life. He was a philosopher king. His people were happier than most in that era of temporal geography.

They had some sentries and soldiers but not enough by far. Another king, simply eager to take from others, found a way for his army to get to them. The battle was fierce even so but in the end the invading soldiers won.

The good king was bound to his throne, now moved outside. The invading king sat freely in another throne, elevated on a hill overlooking the captive king. All those surviving the battle gathered to watch.

The invader king motioned to what looked like a parade to march between the two thrones. The first to pass held the severed head of the good king's wife. He saw this but sat upright with no expression on his face. Those closest saw his muscles clench but clearly he was not about to give the invader king any satisfaction. Next came a procession of the invading soldiers, each waving the severed head of the good king's children. Again no response from the bound king. The crowd was increasingly impressed by his resolve, his iron strength in the face of such tragedy. Next came the heads of his closest friends. Still no response as he suppressed his grief with great will.

Lastly, lagging behind the bloody parade, came a giant invader soldier holding the severed head of the bound king's dog. It was barely past puppyhood and still beautiful even in this setting of horror. At this last, the king's resolve ended and he sobbed loudly.

On hearing this story, the Greek audience debated whether the king cried for the pet because he cared more for it than all the rest, or whether it was just the final hurt to release the whole suppressed anguish for all the decapitated victims. No resolution of this debate expected, they did decide on a name for the good royal: King Henosis.

I was in the body of an elder Greek named for Henosis. My Henosis was a famous actor though most felt was well past his prime. Still, this Henosis had resources and launched a Greek Tragedy for the stage to replay this sad story from their distant past. Further, he insisted on playing the young king, despite his older age. It was to be the peak of his acting career. And so it was.

There on the stage I sat bound to a throne, as now I am the aged actor. I reached the point of explosive grief at last. Drawing on all the pain and disappointment of my life, I sobbed loud enough to reach every Greek in that audience. In the midst of this theatrical triumph, a woman's voice came from the sky: *"Wake up! Everything is okay now!"* A goddess? Interrupting my acting scene's triumph?

No. My wife, being a helpful dream catcher. And so I woke.

Clearly, the aged Greek actor in the dream was me, a writer in his 80s revisiting the time statues of his life. Even the painful ones. Living them in stories as on a stage. But the rest? King Henosis?

The next morning I learned that the name *"Henosis"* was what the ancient Greeks called seeing the essence of things, a unity with nature, with the universe. Some, who have had a stroke impacting logical Procrustean left brain activity, or have had training to pause left brain activity, then may experience a right brain experience that becomes one with all the family of life. In this way our language has kept King Henosis living on as a guide to us.

Beyond local space and time, send him thanks and comfort when he needed it most.

I had no idea I would meet him in person and soon.

Leadville

Theme: *The Mountains High* (Dick and Dee Dee)

Leadville, Colorado, is the highest incorporated town in America. In the 19th century it was the most populated city in the state after Denver. Doc Holliday had his last job as the law there then. Mining, especially silver, brought people there and to a slightly lower neighboring town three miles away in a town named Climax. They've heard all the jokes.

Even today tourists still go to Leadville. From Denver, already a mile high, they drive a few hours uphill to Salida, a name meaning *"exit"*, and truly depart any 'flatlander' geography as they drive ever higher, past Climax, to enter Lake County and finally Leadville.

Of course, most of the year the cold weather centered on Leadville might block this trip. Crisp snow then hugs the city. Or did, but the global warming may yet make Leadville a great place to be. For now, our tourists arrive in the summer. Still cooler than most places, refreshing. Just don't stay in the sun for long. The UV rays at that altitude can burn you quickly. Too much exposure, for some only minutes, could be dangerous, lethal.

Let's assume these tourists are young and athletic. They don't worry about the sun. With full confidence they look for residents to show off their visitor skills. Not hard to find some senior citizen residents to challenge in a run or for a tennis match.

The seniors are used to the thin air at that elevation, the young tourists are not. The tourists lose any contest quickly to the seniors, very soon running out of breath.

Maybe a visiting Sherpa could do better but not many others. That's why race horses aren't allowed to compete if raised at high elevation. Mountain animals or people experience sea level as walking in soupy air, excessive oxygen. Their stronger lungs, greater strength, supplies a huge advantage. Flatlanders used to swimming in abundantly thick air have altitude weakness or even sickness on the mountains.

Still, the view here is great. Even better, at more than 10,000 feet above sea level, you can still see peaks 4,000 feet higher.

Leadville is as far as tourists usually go, but if we actually travel to one of those peaks, we can find a small town nestled in the protective embrace of two mountains.

The people are friendly, having very few visitors, so, after a rest and a great meal, one takes us to what they think we came to see. They are right.

Introductions

Our guide is the Mayor. I'm a semi-retired clinical psychologist. Today, I'm just a tourist on a vacation trip. Sort of.

My companion is a past client of my psychotherapy practice. Let's call him 'Andrew' since that's what his parents did. In Andrew's last visit he thanked me for a successful intervention and used the confidentiality of the meeting to share the existence of this place. He knew I would keep they key town name, and exact directions there secret if I said I would. I did so. He also wanted me to experience something wonderful there as a thank you. Finally, he told me it would be okay to share some of this trip with the world in my writing if I chose. So, as we walk, I quietly record these thoughts.

Another introduction of an individual will be forthcoming soon.

If Andrew is right.

Cemetary

The town cemetary is just ahead.

But first we must walk through a forest path to get there. Maybe another photo will help.

DREAMS AND TIME STATUES

Trees are living beings.

I no longer pluck their leaves while on our way.

This way. On this path.

I thank them, wish them well. Moving on, I recall that live-in milkman, Bob, stepping out on our Nova Scotia home's balcony each night to address any audience (or none). Quoting always the same Robert Frost poem: *"The woods are lovely, dark and deep. But I have promises to keep, and miles to go before I sleep."* And sleep then he would.

Almost there now, says Andrew.

Once the ghost sun is all but gone, the transition to moonlight changed the forest color.

Somwhat misty now. Hard to focus.

The sun is setting. The forest light is suddenly amazing.

This is the ghost moment for the sun.

The actual sun has set but light takes a little time to show us that.

The interim here in this moment is dramatic.

Worth another photo.

And now we come to more hidden cemetary.

As we enter, I stow the camera on my phone.

There is a lone building overlooking this cemetary.

On a hill with a set of stairs.

We take the stairs.

At the top we see that the building is a mausoleum.

It has a doorbell.

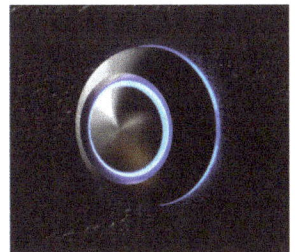

Which is glowing.

Andrew rings the doorbell.

Henosis

The heavy door slowly swings open.

A very tall man, powerfully built, with long hair.

He stands in the doorway.

Looks to be in his late twenties but he seems much older.

He gestures us to enter. We do.

We follow him down a long staircase with guard rails. Clearly far underground by a long shot. Temperature comfortable.

Into a well lit antechamber with comfortable chairs. That light just seems to radiate from the walls.

Behind us and further down is what looks like a large theater or meeting place, maybe more after that.

He sits facing us and we sit as well, finding the chairs comfortable, reassuring.

Andrew was silent looking very respectful. Then he turned to me. Said quietly that we would now make our contribution.

Our host speaks. *"Call me Luke. I know Andrew of course and, with your permission, I would like to know you."*

I nodded yes and meant to speak. But was swallowed in a warm black cloud,

I woke, not sure how much time had passed. I felt rested, centered, safe.

Luke said *"Welcome back. It was only minutes. So now I know you."*

It should have been concerning but at the time it made sense. Besides I was floating, content, a little tired as one feels after exercise.

He went on. *"I trust you now. I can answer your questions fully, as much as I understand them."*

He smiled and though I had asked no questions, he seemed to know them all.

In fact this began the most incredible dialogue of my life. I never spoke but he each time received the question I thought to ask him. And his answers! The words were given along with visual wrap-arounds- we were there experientially in whatever he was recalling.

Luke continued. *"I was very touched by your compassion for me on the day of my death and transformation. Back in my last torturous human moments of life as what you call King Henosis."*

He paused, giving me time to aborb this. Andrew sat enthralled. So: safe.

Luke, seeing me smile and nod (I was in such an unexpectedly mellow mood!) went on with his explanation. Along with the visual around us.

"The story, for all its millenia of duration, is not far off the mark of reality. We, my people and me, lived on top of a famous Greek mountain. Most of those tribes living below us thought of us as gods. Since we were larger, lived longer, and had discovered more."

"But this fascination led them to spy on us continually, take sides in our disputes, thank us or blame us for things we had nothing to do with. Much of their gossip eventually emerged in a blind Greek poet's stories. Oral histories well distorted. Mixed in with an ancient battle between what are now called Turks and Greeks."

The Snake People

Theme: *Snake Farm* Ray Wylie Hubbard

"But at the time just before my own battle, my brother had established his own small kingdom. Snake worshippers. It was not far below us. They envied our greater success. Some of what you might call giants, survivors from Mars (yes, they too had a mass extinction). With the assistance of these large allies, my brother invaded."

"Actually, we repelled them. Not once but many times. I was urged to carry the battle to them and end it. No, I wanted family peace. A mistake. In the end they won. With our own surviving people watching from a distance, they did execute my family in front of me. Including my lifelong wolf companion. I was overwhelmed. My heart was shutting down. I knew I was seconds away from death. "

Here Luke paused to hand me a photo copy. "This is a small descendant of my wolf, what you now call dogs. His heart had stopped after being hit by a car. One of Andrew's daughters brought his body to me, hoping I could help. Well, the little one had not been dead for long so he was easy for me to revive. The girl told me her animal friend was named Arnold, took this picture of us."

"Yes, you can keep the photo. Use it as you will. Privacy matters little now as our own mass extinction has begun its middle phase."

I naturally wanted to know more about this mass extinction phase. But Luke decided to come back to his history lesson. So this is the photograph he gave me.

Luke continued: *"The oral history that you knew ends too soon. Actually, confronted by my brother and all his soldiers, smirking over the bodies of my innocent family, I felt overcome with rage. Though I was tied tightly to my throne, the bonds fell away. Yet I could not move. My own body was limp, left behind, as my spirit rushed these killers in a tsunami wave of energy. The wave swallowed their energy- I know no other way to describe it. They, every one, fell to ashes."*

" *"It was too late to save my family. My energy wave, magnified by what I had absorbed from the invaders, returned to my now dead body. Entered and revived me as something else."*

"My heart and lungs then functioned as did my brain but all were powered by this energy wave, further magnified by the energy taken

from the invaders. In time I realized that this was my food. No longer did I care about ingestion, digestion, excretion, or normal physical processes of human life."

"I rose from the throne, radiating new life. Stepped forward. But my own people, watching this from a higher point, ran. Terrified."

"Yes, I was called a vampire or worse. But blood was not needed. Over time I learned to absorb small amounts of energy from volunteers in exchange for answering questions or otherwise helping."

"Where did I go? I wandered down past the flatlanders and eventually to the ocean. You wouldn't know this of mountain people but we were born in water. My own mother had me in a water birth. We always loved to swim. So I joined the dolphins for a lifetime or so."

"Dolphins are a higher lifeform. Playful. Yet with larger more advanced brains. By mutual consent dolphins can share direct experience- to be in the world through each other's senses. A version of which I am doing with you now. And their spoken language! Fast high pitched concentrations of so much, stories, feelings, music. I learned so much from them! In the end though, I went on back to the human world."

"Where? The next stop was Egypt. Such advanced chemical and biological science, farther along than is found today. Their morality not so much- slavery, autocracy, war. Genetic experiments blending animal DNA into people. Tragic. A few of these mixes did survive and were worshipped. They were not happy. And then the visitors that came from ... Another story. I digress. I did keep wandering, creating a presence in generation after generation, always wandering."

"Oh. I see your other questions are accumulating. Thank you for your restraint. I will answer some more now."

"Oh no, I don't miss the taste of food. With the consent of my energy donors, I also retain certain gift memories, especially wonderful food tastes among them. I only share what is given freely but my guests are quite generous."

"Another question? No, you don't need to speak them out loud. You have a strong mind. Infact your questions are quite loud as I receive them."

"Mass extinction? Oh you know about that. The euphemism is 'climate change' or even 'global warming'. It is caused by human greed of the wealthiest. Its termed by scientists as the 'Anthropocene", a human-caused mass extinction, well under way."

"Oh. What can I do to help? Not much at this point. Though I do love the story told about Saint Francis walking on the beach with a friend and seeing thousands of little sea creatures washed up to die there on land. Francis began tossing some back to ocean survival, one at a time. His friend told him that what he was doing wouldn't matter since there were thousands more breathing their last on the sand than any one person could throw back. Francis held up another one and said 'It matters to this one', tossing the lucky survivor back into the ocean. I'm no Saint Francis but I can at least save the people of this town and even those in Leadville."

"Many decades ago, I bought this hill and the Mausoleum on it. With a view of a cemetary and considering the climate, the purchase was a bargain. It included all the land below which, turns out, is an extensive mountain with caves, air pockets, and an underground stream of water. Goes on for miles."

"So under this hill, work is continually extending living quarters large enough for the survival of those living in this region. Underground is a constant room temperature. At this elevation and in this within-mountain home, we should be free from the flood and fire. At least for a generation or several. Does it matter? Yes, it does to them. And to me."

"I did of course put in a doorbell so local visitors could come by. When I am open to such visits it will glow as it did today for you and Andrew."

"What powers that I have discovered that might help? Well, there is my form of time travel."

"Yes, travel in time. Within yourself. I see that in your clinical practice you once had a patient who trusted nobody, not even you, but desperatelly needed advice for some essential life choices. Through hypnosis you connected her to an older version of herself. In this way she gave herself good advice and best choices were made."

" You also are aware of, umm, the theory of your good friend William Braud that healing the adult of trauma can ripple back in time to healing that adult as a child. Thinking of things in that way can lead you to time travel."

"Through meditation, hypnosis, safe hallucinogen substances, other ways, one can go back in time to yourself at a younger age. Look through their eyes, assist them in key choices. Yes, I have done this. Yes, my own unique energy state makes it easier. But I do think that living humans can learn to do this."

"Have I done it? Yes. I did assist some later Hebrew tribes write a portion of their history scrolls. Its where I got the name Luke from."

DREAMS AND TIME STATUES

"Why don't I go back to my younger self as King Henosis and save my family? Ah, I wish! But then I would never have transformed, so a paradox. I've tried but I keep being snapped back to the present."

"Yes, a past without the paradox can be diverted or improved but one needs to be very cautious. Do these statues in time change for the better? If not, are we just creating a different multiverse? Maybe worse?"

" Oh! Yes, I see you tried this travel back to a younger self in the 1970s. Just visual though. Seeing yourself in the mirror at a younger age. Hmm. True, now you look into a mirror wondering if an older self is looking back (laughter). Creepy huh?"

"Have I left anything out of my own history that I would like to tell you? What a kind question! Let me consider this."

"Well, yes. As I've shown you, my people who had seen me destroy my brother and his troops were so frightened of me that I had to leave them to wander my own path about the earth. So many lives."

"The descendants of my brother's family, from those that had not invaded, eventually told a lie to the Greek and Hebrew tribes. A version stolen from the story of the Romulus and Remus brothers."

"Said that since I had killed my own brother, I had been condemned by Zeus (and his son Jezeus) to wander the earth forever. Made people hate me as well as fear. My brother was the aggressor, not me."

"The Hebrew tribes paid me a tribute by placing a tribal mark on my arm. The lie from my brother's descendants claimed it was a mark of divine condemnation for his death. Not to long ago I covered it over with a tatoo better expressing my truth."

Luke handed me another photo, this time of his tatoo:

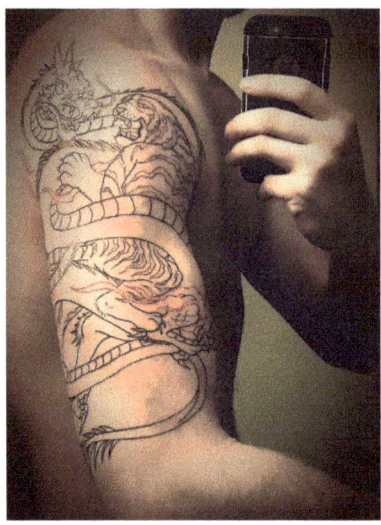

"It combines the dragon and tiger branches of my existence. Indigenous myths in what is now called England refer to Arthur as a Pendragon or son of a dragon."

"A Romanian saga remembers its king as a dragon or "Dracul" in that language. His more famous son is simularly referred to as the son of this dragon or, in Romanian, "Dracula"."

"The tiger represents my Chinese family line and a more admirable brother there."

" Yes, I may have been more involved in all of these during my own wanderings. How I might have been involved, well, another day, another conversation."

"For now, we can see the dragon and tiger eclipsing that prior mark I carried for far too long. One so misunderstood. Good riddance."

"Finally, I also took my brother's name from those Hebrew and Christian tribe's unjust myth about me. Giving me that hostile name, a target for the world. So I took that brother's ancient name as my own last name. Just to further defuse the issue."

"With that substitution, my name is now officially 'Luke Abel'. Maybe an extra 'L'?"

"Anyway, never again will I be called 'Cain'."

Mother Duck Society

Theme: *Sasha's music in Peter and the Wolf* Sergei Prokofiev

The Mother Duck Society or MDS began as early as the year 2030.

It claimed all of humanity as members but was said to have been founded by a group of media-savvy teens. Ones professing to love duck motherhood such that they constantly referred to themselves and selected others as *"Mother Duckers"*. Yelled with zest.

By that year, survivors had more serious problems to address so nobody objected.

The true surprise was when MDS revealed itself as artificial intelligence. The AI was just proving that it had a sense of humor.

Maybe off-the-mark but still, sure and certain evidence that it had evolved closer to human. Devolved?

Of course by then there were no ducks left anyway.

The Next Big Thing

Theme: *Mothra, A Deusa Selvagem* 1961

It began with his childhood love for the 26 blind swordsman *Zatoichi* movies, all played by Shintaro Katsu.

Of course they had begun in 1962, long before he was born. But he grew up in Hollywood during a revival.

Now an adult, he had the highly paid responsibility to invent the next big thing for televised wrestling. Following a substantial drought of ideas, he refreshed himself by watching one of his *Zatoichi* DVDs. Binged quite a few in fact. Zatoichi *always* won.

And so could he. Finally accepting the brilliance of his thought, he presented his idea and it was accepted. The blind wrestler *Zato Itchy* became a TV hit. Since TV wrestling is scripted in advance,

Zato's constant pre-ordained wins were also acknowledged for his impressive ring acrobatics.

And then the day came along when the script called for him to lose. His sighted opponent had a light-tight blindfold put on. And (after many rehearsals) Zato lost as required.

By then a group of the next generation of teen wrestling viewers had adopted the fad of fighting blindfolded. Swords, knives, fists, guns. It caught on, made the news here and there.

Meanwhile our wrestling promotor, devoid of any other fresh ideas, had been let go. He was in luck though, winding up as the hired promoter for the 2028 Summer Olympics. The TV ratings for 2024 in Paris had been inadequate for their corporate sponsors, especially that unfortunate swim event in the river Seine which had received raw sewage contributions from Parisians for centuries.

Still without any new ideas, he called again on an old one. The last big thing. So it was that the 2028 Summer Olympics had such modified events as the blindfolded javelin throw, the blindfolded shotput, not mention blindfolded archers and gun shootings.

Well, the TV ratings were indeed up for all these though live audience bystanders were not as frequent as before. More frequent of course were the very expensive lawsuits.

He suggested using actual blind athletes in one Olympic fencing contest. The try-outs were rather bloody, even for referees and the one unfortunate vendor. But once actual blind athletes were finally found and admitted, they were so good that sighted fencers refused to compete with them. Got them diverted to the 2032 Paralympics.

He needed another big thing. He thought that sometimes two failures can be merged to make a success.

So he staged a country event back in Paris for the final week. A men's swimming competition in the Seine.

At the 2024 Olympics, the historic river portion flowing through Paris had been cleaned to more or less safe for swimming. But by 2028 the factories had renewed pollution.

Further, a Parisian youth gang, inspired by one in the USA, had begun defecating into the Seine upstream from the city. Calling it *"Sending our boats to Paris"*.

So even stinkier now than before, enough Olympic swimmers still dared to compete and the event took place.

TV ratings complied, up and up.

Three medalists did finish and made the awards stand. Fully aware of the fragrance coming from each other, all were mercifully granted nose plugs.

The press, with its usual wit, at least halfway there, named this competition event as *"In-Seine"*.

Unfortunately, the lawsuits and several unfortunate funerals led to the promoter once again being fired, with near deadly prejudice, plus global disdain. He went home to Hollywood where he retired, incognito, and at peace.

At first.

That teen gang of blindfolded fighters had spread as new generations came up and the original teens aged out. One branch just blindfolded their victims but this, for some reason was considered unsportsmanlike.

But not before our promoter had perished in this version of his next big thing.

The majority of the teen gang had adopted a name and an identity.

They were called the **FY**s, a name many mistook for cursing. The gang itself knew the **FY** stood for *"Fascist Youth"*.

By now they were politically connected, many on their way to leadership in the *Great Again* one of the two major national political parties.

White Power

Themes: *Walk on the Wild Side* Jimmy Smith instrumental; *Gonna Feel Much Better When You're Gone* Buffy Saint-Marie

Madison Avenue still talks about it. Sudden revelation for an obvious unforgettable slogan exactly fitting products selling themselves as whitening. A game changer. A winner: *"**White Power**"*

It was shopped to the teeth whitener companies first.

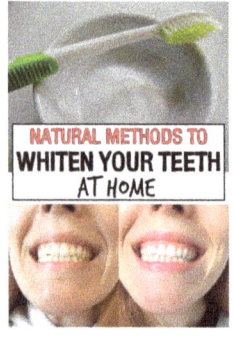 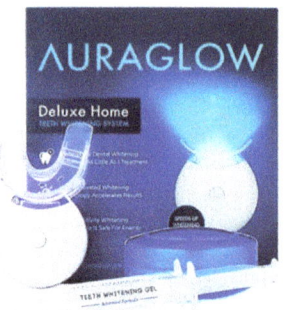 

But they said "NO!"

Twice for emphasis:

Then it was shopped to the clothes whitening detergent companies.

But they refused too.

Then the *White Power* slogan was offered to the Skin Whitener companies:

Including

And

Yet again even these companies said

Go Away!

On a tip the slogan was offered to a related global company:

The answer was emphatic.

Time to reconsider strategy.

An idea came from reading a book about birds.

Producing white poop in large quantities come naturally to our numerous avian cousins.

It is in fact living proof of the slogan- True *White Power.*

Not always received with delight.

DREAMS AND TIME STATUES

Sometimes with educational aspects.

Or sure and certain divine insight:

Following this unexpected lead, a very smart gray parrot capable of speech and strategy was paid as a consultant.

With answers.

This led them to bring their previously so unwanted *White Power* slogan to, finally, a welcome place.

The 2024 MAGA-devoted SCOTUS Gang of Six

Purchase accomplished.

SCOTUS Moon

Themes: *Moon over Miami* Anita Bryant; *That's Amore* Dean Martin

Historians tell us that confidentiality finally ended on or before the year 2024 in the United States of America. That was when the photos and videos in medical records of famous people were hacked. Their publicists soon distributed the better booty views of their clients, retouched as needed, on print media and the international internet everywhere. Opposition researchers soon counter-distributed unflattering posterior and other intimate views of celebrity targets, now including politicians and world leaders, with emphasis on the throwback Supreme Court of the United States (SCOTUS).

Many years later, a US president attempted to make light of this historical situation by repeatedly saying "The urology associations couldn't stop the flow" and "Proctology lawsuits couldn't stop downloads". Her impeachment failed by only one vote, only the second time in history.

More recently, a prominent sociologist, uninhibited by any need for formal evidence, pulled from his usual orificial source a more specific origin of this end of the 2024 'Age of Innocence'.

This is that story.

The Beginning

During the highly infectious pandemic of the early 2020s, remote electronic communications like *zoom* became commonplace. This also expanded telehealth as a means for doctors to safely meet and examine their patients. It helped cover geographical barriers and keep everybody safe. Even as the years of deadly epidemic crisis receded, the convenience of this approach became a mainstay.

Also ever more effective were the invasive internet hackers. Security protocols were all eventually bypassed by underage geniuses. Some of these had skills far surpassing any yet developed conscience. Accordingly the telehealth examinations were routinely recorded elsewhere with no permission, especially for celebrities and other exalted individuals.

So it was that an offshore outlaw station broadcasting to the Miami region began showing the gynecology exams of female celebrities complete with ornate stirrups.

Following serious threats of lawsuits for sexual harassment, the station changed its focus to a more equally offensive but gender equitable broadcast of proctology exams.

As this caught on, the controversial show, consequently growing to be viewed online across the globe, was regularly broadcast as *"Moon over Miami"*.

With so many affluent dignitaries having their posteriors viewed publically and, worse, humorously, lawsuits did progress at last. The station floated in international waters and had accumulated some superb lawyers of its own. As well as substantial revenue. Even the somewhat related advertising.

Freedom of expression was argued as was public domain for celebrities. Even some of the celebrity publicists supported these viewings. Particularly when the reviews were favorable. Or controversial. Lawsuits were either won by the station or, if not, were just

On to Congress

Political and government officials were another matter. With more easily wounded egos, their indignation rippled through Congress. For example, Representative Marjorie Taylor Greene made some humorously intended remarks about Senator Graham's bottom, focusing on hair dispersion and poor hygiene. The good senator held a press conference attacking Congressperson Greene and the station. He said the show *Moon over Miami* was *"way too gay"*.

Representative Greene's responses cannot be reprinted here. In a rare bipartisan show of support for another woman, Representative Alexandria Ocasio-Cortez urged Greene to rise above the senator's remarks, saying *"Graham is just a cracker"*.

The show's ratings rose again. As did its resources. The attorneys for Senator Graham, using his gluteus maximus as the test case, did manage to advance past level after level of defeat to finally appeal the show's existence to the U.S. Supreme Court.

Enter SCOTUS

Even after many years from their appointment, lifetime serving justices continued their presence as Supremes. Their protected conservative super majority led pundits to predict that the court would find for Senator Graham.

The show had a remedy in waiting. It had acquired some secret footage from one of the SCOTUS justices and this now could be released. There had been a rumor that Justice Clarence Thomas secretly followed the show. That he had managed to acquire some proctology material on another justice. The online speculation was that his highly confidential booty illustration material was that of the youngest female justice, Amy Vivian Coney Barrett.

While this eventually proved to be true at a much later date, the majority of the Justice Thomas derriere archives, hacked and hijacked by a gifted eight year old, were revealed to be of Chief Justice John Roberts. *Moon over Miami* immediately broadcast these with accompanying thanks to Justice Thomas. Justice Thomas, when asked for comment, stated that he had kept the proctology material only out of his high admiration for the Chief Justice and his long leadership while sitting on the bench.

Justice Neil Gorsuch was eventually found to have had substantial intimate common cause with the wives of Justices Alito and Thomas. Out of this productive misconduct lucrative flag sales emerged, all on the theme of husband booty and making their anus great again.

Justice Samuel A. Alito struck back by blaming his spouse for all his past unpopular decisions on the court as well as for various ongoing global wars. She responded by scheduling a press conference to reveal what his middle initial "A" stood for.

Further, annoyed by her husband's demand that she take down their MAGA coup-friendly flags, substituted her bras and panties flying on the flag poles of both homes. Alito vetoed this as well.

Consequently she responded at each location with custom flags of her husband's derriere photos, well flanked with his sewed-in actual inside-out stained briefs.

A top national newspaper's Arts Section reviewed these last flags with photographs and *"Justice Alioto's briefs clearly resemble a Jackson Pollock style flag smeared with Grey Poupon mustard and melted pinto beans. A stylistic triumph"*

The Departures

Justice Gorsuch stepped away from the struggle to resign from the court. He disappeared from public view, as did the wives of Justices Alito and Thomas who joined him, followed by the unannounced addition of Mrs. Roberts to his growing harem. Rumors ran from salacious to Dateline television crime but the mystery of what and why remains even to this day.

The youngest SCOTUS justices, Amy Coney Barrett and Brett Kavanaugh, worked together for a more contemporary response. Inspired by Mrs. Alito's original flags, they took external shots of each of them bending over, robes raised, mooning their bare exits, on both t-shirts and flags. Sold like their also marketed butt-shaped hotcakes.

Kavanaugh added a premium upgrade photo of his own rectal boofing to television ads ("Find a hole and Fill It") for his favorite beer. Its celebrated usage during years of Pride parades may not have given him consolation. The worst of it for him was his appearance promoting his ad in Buffalo where he was booed and pelted with ripe fruit for insisting to call the city "Boofalo".

The three liberal justices on SCOTUS caucused to consider this chaos. Justice Elena Kagan suggested they copyright their own proctology photos to prevent undue exposure. Justice Sonia Sotomayor creatively suggested they instead collect their proctology photos quickly and place them in a time capsule with an unlisted end date. Justice Ketanji Brown Jackson reminded them that none of them had any proctology photos to hide. Further, she pointed out that as older women, not to mention race and ethnicity, the media had already done an impressive job of hiding their existence and clearly brilliant decisions on SCOTUS. Counting on this, camouflage seemed the best anonymous path forward. Agreement.

This plan worked so well that the press never noticed when they resigned from the openly corrupt court. Each of them, at the urging of Ari Melber, Rachel Maddow, and Joy Reid, became popular hosts at MSNBC.

All the attention at the time went to the resignations of Alito and Thomas. They formed a private equity giant built on accumulated funds received over the years from billionaires having their interests before the court. Unfortunately, all was lost in their disastrous Global Payday Loan scandal with the Trump family. The subsequent lighthearted Thomas pubic hair ads for Pepsi failed to help.

This left SCOTUS with only three justices. The Senate was deadlocked on any new appointments.

With all the controversy, the Supreme Court did not any longer have the minimum of the four justices needed to hear the case against Moon over Miami. This allowed the show to continue unmolested by any further legal challenges. Chief Justice John Roberts himself had made the refusal. He had no comment for press at the time.

His eventual autobiography though absolved Justice Thomas of any fault in this matter, noting that his own nether region had been well groomed and definitely ready for prime time. He did apologize for his prior constant pointing to the seat of his robes and saying to the other deliberating justices "Smell that dairy air!"

Given the hopeless nature of jurisprudence for SCOTUS, Roberts finally left with the other two justices. His tenure at the Trump Presidential Library on Alcatraz was unremarkable.

Justices Barrett and Kavanaugh remained unknown in our historical record though the X-rated rumors were legendary.

Historian journalists have recently found evidence that they did wind up in Alabama, Kavanaugh on its Supreme Court.

Barrett was there as well, but in opposition to him, she headed the state Child Protective Services (CPS) so as to rescue the IVF frozen children, aka eggs, from a sure and certain cold demise.

Next

We all know how the climate runaway death of our planet was reversed at the last moment by the world coalition of science led by United Nations Secretary-General Obama. But it was her husband Barack instead that was called back to the USA by the newly elected Democratic President and Congress to lead and reconstitute SCOTUS. This time with a real code of ethics. All three MSNBC former liberal justices returned as justices in the new, very new, SCOTUS, along with the subsequently appointed justices Maddow, Melber, Reid, and Charlamagne tha God.

The eight year old who had hacked Justice Thomas was eventually offered a seat as an NSA analyst with competing bids from the CIA, the Secret Service, the Pentagon, and, for some reason, the United States Postal Service. At the time he chose instead to continue his grade school education.

But by his sixth grade graduation he had become Station Chief of the top rated global show *"Moon over Miami"*.

In an interview with the station owners, they defended his tender age: *"He's been just great for our bottom line."*

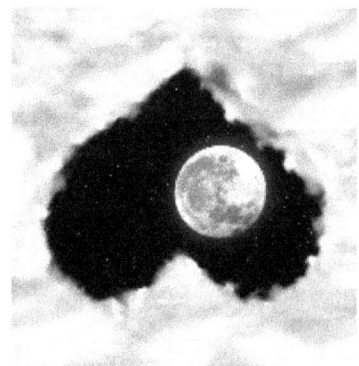

Note: *As a nod to attorneys, it is clarified here that this and the one before it is a fictional SCOTUS story. It did not happen. Yet.*

E Pluribus Union

Theme: *My Baby* Ken Nordine (with Fred Astaire & Barrie Chase)

E pluribus unum, not union, is on the USA currency. It means "out of many, one" and signifies the original 13 colonies banding together to form a country. A deeper meaning is that this unifying strategy is a powerful adaptation basis for survival. Not only for the human family but for all living things. Each of us begins with a single fertilized cell, winding up with a cohesive conglomeration of cellular unity, a body we live in. That same principle applies to our social organizations. We collaborate with others to accomplish a unified purpose, a union. Now: unions around common goals are known in labor circles, in federated countries, and in nature. Trees collaborate, as do wolves, dolphins, ants, bees, birds, dogs. What if this collaboration for us and ours began even earlier than we thought? Might be interesting to speculate.

The Baby Union (BU) (pronounced *"Boo!"*)

Maintaining the benefits of infancy is central here. Survival yes, but much much more. Oil massage, diaper change with powder, intimate access to breast nourishment. Automatic garbage disposal 24/7. Piggy back transport, free everything, sleep at will, play on own schedule.

Tax free. A kind of very early retirement before any actual work. Handicap status. Dues not collected.

The problem for this union of course is continuity. The leadership ages out way too fast.

But while the membership qualifies, its communications can be very effective. Complaints are ordinarily heard and responded to. And once in contact with other members, solidarity possible. The volume of request from several babies in tandem is exponentially powerful.

Strikes include food on the floor, fasting, upchucking, and more insistent forms of protest. Public image and impact very successful from overwhelming cuteness.

Babies can have powerful alliances and connections with the adult network. Legislation follows. The BU demands to be taken into consideration.

The Puppy Union (PU) (pronounced *"Pee You!"*)

Man's best friend is formidably unified from the beginning. Born with litter mates, they collaborate immediately. Blessed with even more cuteness than those in the BU, they achieve the same benefits. In addition their inter-communication is enhanced by powerful hearing and smell. A simple walk in the park tells each one much about the other members- what they had for breakfast, who's available for a date, and where to contribute to the nourishment of trees or the cleansing of hydrants. They know where to sniff and are unfussy eaters. They do exercise their humans as a regular responsibility. They protect as needed. A two-way exchange. Again free dues.

Here too, the problem for this union is continuity. The leadership and the members age out even faster than those in the BU.

So

Please show your support for those in either union. Members grow into larger beings, often in good standing with more powerful associations.

Lately in the BU, they have been experiencing increased pressure from segments of their grown human members. Pressure to provide even better privileges and recognition to a union membership where some may be as small as a single cell.

This would be the Fetus Union (FU) (pronounced *"Eff You!"*).

The Porch Pirate Surprise

Theme: *Great Pretender* Platters; *Little Blue Riding Hood* Stan Freberg

Fill it with a week's worth of fragrant evacuation.

Full and ready, the *Cologuard* box waits to be stolen.

Porch Pirate gift box to girlfriend lacks desired effect.

Howland Owl, Practicing Proctologist

Themes: *This is the End* Doors; *Constipation Blues* Screamin' Jay Hawkins;

Howland Owl was inspired by a proctology webinar to follow this path. His goal is to join the World Health Organization or the WHO (pronounced *"Hoo!"* by him). For this he needs media visibility of his Medical prowess. Here he has graduated from navel oranges to ambrosia apples. The rest of the fruit has hidden in the refrigerator except for the bananas that are now getting ideas.

The Room

Themes: *Smoke on the Water* Deep Purple; *Where's the Money?* Dan Hicks

This below was a dream but here's the part that really happened in an earlier time: In the "Summer of Love" my brother was getting his mail at the Blue Unicorn in San Francisco. I had time between planes to visit him there. They claimed that they had never heard of him. Turned out that they thought I was police since I was wearing shoes with laces. Then, at another time, one of our uncles was close to his death. Of our uncles and aunts on that side of

the family, he was the only one who had no spouse or children. No immediate beneficiaries. He had a million dollars to leave. His older brother, Manny, volunteered to disperse his money to their brothers, sisters, and their children while he was still alive to appreciate it. So it was. I and my brother received $5,000 twice in two different installments. Our father, the uncle's brother, got twice that.

The Dream

It was winter. I was walking through the snow to visit my brother and give him his mail with the two $5,000 checks.

He was staying in a university dorm for courses offered during this seasonal break.

I had been on a shuttle to get to his dorm but it broke down. I spent a lot of time trying to find his place on foot but, as dream luck would have it, I saw him and he took me there.

By then it was night. He could get me a dorm room in the morning but in the meantime, he found a special room I could stay in.

It had been the Janitor's place. But the university had laid off half the janitors including this one so his room became a store room. Boxes stacked against one wall.

It was a large room with an adjacent basic bathroom. It had a refrigerator and hotplate, dishes. But…

In the middle of the room was a California king size mattress, covers. The room lights were from low light lamps. Next to the mattress was a little bar.

My brother explained that this had become the sex room for all four dorm floors. Couples could use the room for as much as an hour and then it was somebody else's turn. An hour timer was on the bar to regulate this. When the room was in use, a DO NOT DISTURB sign would be hung outside the door.

Except on one day a week when staff would come to clean, change the sheets in every dorm room including this one. Everybody knew to not use the special room on that morning. Tomorrow.

Morning came and I was out of the room in time. We had breakfast in another building. Coming back to the dorm, we noticed a DO NOT DISTURB sign on the room's door.

My brother needed to get to his class so I agreed to let the unexpected couple know they had to get out before cleaning staff got there.

I knocked and entered. The door hadn't been locked.

Inside was a young woman nursing her baby. A boy of about six moved between us to protect her. They looked like immigrants without papers, as they in fact were.

I wasn't expecting any of this.

I told the boy I was just there to get them away safely before the cleaning staff got there. He translated to his mother and she smiled. Gathered her things and children, followed me to where I was now staying. A room already cleaned.

The boy said his mother had asked him to speak for them since her English was poor. Of course, my Spanish was not much more than some insults I had learned in Nuevo Laredo during my military days.

In that border town, I had also learned how amazingly bright the young street children were. Many even much younger than this boy could sell things, make change, conduct effective conversation in two or more languages. So I sat and listened to this boy with respect. Here's what he said.

"Thank you dear patron for your kind assistance to my small family."

His mother spoke to him quietly in Spanish. He nodded and went on.

"My mother would like me to explain our presence here. We lived in a small town not far from Nuevo Laredo. We have family on the Texas side in Laredo. My mother and father grew up near each other. They were already best friends as children. Agreed to marry and have a family together when they grew up. This they did."

"By then our father had become big, strong. This was good. By then my mother had become very beautiful, as you see. This was not good for us. The cartel near our town might just take our mother away if they saw her and, if we fight them about it, kill us."

"So my mother kept out of sight as much as possible when I was born and grew up. Her mother gave her a black veil to carry if needed so cartel soldiers would think she was a widow. And when my little sister was growing inside her, they might just think she was fat."

"But when this baby here was born, a cartel soldier noticed her before she came home from the hospital. Followed her. My father was bigger and discouraged him from coming into our house. The cartel soldier said he would be back with his friends."

"My father understood this, this danger to us. The cartel soldiers had killed people we knew for less. It was decided to move across

the border to our family in Laredo. My father paid a coyote to learn where we might get under the Texas razor wire to safely cross the Big River."

"That night we waded into the Rio Grande (you understand the Spanish name? Yes?) at the exact spot. The moon was big and much light was there to guide us."

"It also guided the cartel soldier and two of his people with him. Right behind us. Trying to catch up."

"But my father found the right spot first. He had my mother and her baby swim under the wire where there was room and helped them reach the shore. He came back for me and made sure I started to get across safely too. But by then the cartel soldiers had caught up. To keep them from dragging me back he told me to keep going as fast as I could, to join my mother and sister."

"I did as I was told, got to them at the shore. Looking back we could see that he had beat them. Two were swimming back to the Mexico side, blood in the water. One was caught in the razor wire and wasn't moving. But my father was caught too and, struggle as he might, the water kept closing over his face. He was drowning. Blood, his or the other man's, clouded around him."

"I saw two United States Federales, customs soldiers watching from the shore. I begged them to save our father's life, said he was not cartel. My mother joined in. Maybe she was more persuasive. The two Federales ran to the river to save him. But the Texas state soldiers would not let them pass."

"Our father died there and then in the water, in the razor wire."

"The Texas soldiers took us to a bus. By then our mother was wearing her black widow's veil for real so they took little notice of us. Said we were going to a city where we would be cared for, safe."

"Many long hours later the bus emptied us out in a place far from home, no family there. Cold winter. A woman on the bus had given her large winter coat to my mother where all three of us could huddle and be warm. Nice except for all her tears with baby sister crying too. Maybe a little bit from me, maybe, I don't remember."

"We saw the university on a hill. Thought we might be safe near all those young people. Found this building and this empty room here. Where you saw us."

"Go back to the family we have in Laredo? My mother says never! The Texas soldiers let our father die! No, we must somehow settle in this cold snowy place."

"But you know? I think this will be our lucky place, even so. We will MAKE IT our lucky place. A very good future is here. If we take it."

Plus, we live, we have each other. And we have the extra luck right now of your great kindness. A plan? No, not yet."

I had a plan for them though. The boy translated for his mother.

I would take them to a safe place, a hotel. From there I would connect them with a good immigration lawyer to apply for asylum status. But first I had some resources for them.

I took one of my envelopes with my own $5,000 in it and gave it to the boy to give to his mother. For her family to settle in to this cold strange place and make it home.

He explained this to her and she seemed surprised, thankful, then hopeful, a little.

Then I took the second envelope out, the one with my other $5,000. This I gave to the brilliantly capable boy. To keep as his own.

Told him I had no idea what he would do with this money but I knew he would use it well, protect his family. Build that lucky future.

I gave him my contact information so I could follow his progress.

I think likely the beginning of a new American dynasty.

And I woke up.

Schopenhauer and the Dream

Theme: *Rhapsody in Blue* George Gershwin

3 AM. My body was at rest, asleep.

But I was on stage suddenly in the middle of a group receiving last minute directions from the director. Mostly just *"Wing it!"*

The curtains opened, bright lights for us but the audience not seen, smoky clouds surround the stage. Group interacting, loud dialogue.

I'm approached by the director, now an actor stirring things up.

I grab a red book off an end table and meet him.

Him: *"Reading a book are we?"*

Me: *"A good one! Schopenhauer. Written in the original German."*

H: *"The German philosopher? The sour and grumpy one?"*

M: *"Maybe."*

H: *"You can read German?"*

M: *"Nine."*

H: *"The way you said that sounds like you're not even spelling it right out loud! It's 'Nein' "*

M: *"You sound just like Schopenhauer."*

H: *"I'll bet you can't even spell his name! Can you?"*

M: *"Nein."*

H: *"Can you tell me a single thing about Schopenhauer?*

M: *"He couldn't spell his name either. THAT was the source of his sadness. Much like you. It's in the book."* (Pats book)

H: *"Give me that book!"* (Grabs book.)

M: *"Even if you can read German, it won't tell you anything about Schopenhauer."*

H: *"Why? And I CAN read German. So there!"*

M: *"Still won't help you know anything about Schopenhauer, Shicekopf."*

H: *"That so, Dummkopf?"*

M: *"So! You misheard me. Not about Schopenhauer. It's about classical music."*

H: *"What?"*

M: *"Not about Schopenhauer. It's about the 'Chopin Hour'. On the radio."*

H: *"Shicedrek! Chopin died the century before there WAS any radio."*

M: *"Rerun?"*

H: (Turning to the front of stage) *"AND SCENE!"*

Applause coming from within the clouds in front.

—

Relief as I woke.

This is another story that visited me in the lull between sleep and wake. As a very young child I had read "A Tale of Two Cities", knowing that someday I would write stories too, just like the author. Everybody said I was a little Dickens.

Wagging a Tail of Two Puppies

Theme: *Born to be Wild* Steppenwolf

He was the best of dogs.

He was the wildest of dogs.

They were brothers. Originally named "London" and "Paris" but these were not names they knew.

One litter twin looked identical but had been adopted into a wealthy man's home. Pampered with great food and plush shelter.

But his brother lived in an old carton in the woods. Wild and free. Somebody named him "Sidney" after the address on the carton.

Sidney and his twin double "Charles" were getting too big to be puppies much longer. Nor did Sidney have any jealousy for his twin, living so much better. Sidney enjoyed his freedom. Loved his brother.

The two puppies were so connected that when Charles first had great fear, mixed with sadness, Sidney understood immediately.

The human Charles was living with was coming home soon to take him to the vet. But Charles was not sick. He understood well from an older dog next door that at the vet he was about to be neutered. His masculinity cut off. Why? To make him more friendly? Charles was already the kindest of canines. So he was alarmed.

Sidney had to help him. He dug a large hole under the fence into the manicured lawn of his twin's yard. Easily fit through and pushed into the house through the doggie door made especially for Charles. On his way out, Charles nuzzled his brother with thanks. Had comfort that his wild brother would survive somehow. Freedom had made Sidney more resourceful. And now Charles could live as wild as he had always wished to do.

Once in the house, Sidney knew he was stuck there. The doggie door only opened into the house but not out into the yard. Not into the free world.

A good thing that Sidney on arriving had held the door open long enough for Charles to exit. And then it slammed shut in place behind him. An exit closed. Sidney trotted away from it with a wag of his tail.

Always hopeful as puppies can be, Sidney wandered into the kitchen. His nose took him to a cupboard that had an aroma announcing food. Easy to break into. Sidney stuffed himself with the best meal he had ever had.

Then marked the corners of every room with his liquid signature.

More full than he had ever been, he climbed onto a plush bed. A short happy nap.

Waking, he strolled to the front room's thick green carpet and, as he had always done in the woods, squeezed out the major news of what he had eaten before.

A moment of sadness that no other puppies were there to see and smell his contribution there steaming in the middle of carpet luxury. Yet he had no fear about the looming trip to the vet. Let them guillotine his masculinity. He would live out his life as Charles now, a pampered puppy.

Or maybe not. Once his human would see his contributions to the manor. There would be consequences. The best of which was that his brother Charles was now safe and free. On return, maybe the human would just evict him into the yard wild. Where he could join his brother. Both to be free, wild. It could happen. Or maybe not. But now he had a plan, a hope. Count on it.

Anyway, humans did not understand how impressive Sidney's carpet contribution really was, or so puppies would think. Just awesome. It was the largest and most pungent he had ever brought into the world.

With that he set aside any concern about the human or the vet. Charles was safe. Sidney would endure.

Settling down on the carpet to at least appreciate his massive dropping on his own, he then had this happy puppy thought about it: *"This is a far, far better thing I did than I have ever done before"*.

Then he circled three times, laid down on a very comfortable mat, and rested his head.

It was a far, far better rest than he had ever known.

-

Remembering Dickens back in his 1859 Time Statue location.

Honesty

Theme: *Que Sera Sera* Doris Day; *Banana Boat (Day-O)* Stan Freberg

A common theme from Washington DC or state level grant funders is to help the grant "targets" (interesting word choice) who they refer to as "underserved". A common typo for that word is one that omits the first r and refers to these grant recipients as "undeserved". Unconscious bias? Honesty? Or candor?

There is a big difference between honesty and candor. Honesty is admirable. Essentially it means no intentional lies, increasingly rare in today's media discourse. Candor, on the other hand, is saying everything that's meant, diplomatic or not. Imagine you in the park on a beautiful spring day when you see a young mother you know with her baby in a carriage. In all honesty you might say *"How nice to see you and your baby enjoying this fine day."* In all candor you might also say *"The kid's kind of ugly though with that really big head. And from the smell, I think his diaper needs changing."*

Maybe instead of a dichotomy, we might think of honesty as a continuum with candor at the extreme end of the spectrum. The end that draws the most attention. As with that Texas meteorologist, the honest TV weatherman.

Austin, Texas in the late 2020s

The weather was hard to predict. On the way to the stage he quick opened a window and looked at the sky. Dark clouds at one end, blue sky at the other, getting dark too early- maybe tornadoes? Or not? The excessive mushrooms he just had gave him more than enough confidence to move on. More being the key here.

He rushed to the cameras and found his spot. Countdown to live TV. But. That night the teleprompter wasn't working. This he discovered with seconds to go.

The newscaster introduced him to the live audience as the totally best source for predicting Texas weather. And here he is.

So he improvised.

Shrugging he smiled at the camera and burst into song:

"Que Sera Sera, whatever will be will be, the future's not mine to see, Que Sera Sera"

And he walked off the set.

Visually a sensation throughout internet outlets, it was the beginning of fame for the *'Honest Weatherman'* of Austin, Texas. Candid really.

Clones

The *Que Sera Sera* craze caught on and spread. In an era of blatant lies, the raw candor was found to be refreshing.

Though not always.

There was that famous cardiologist in Atlanta that informed every patient he saw all day that their diagnosis was, shrugging, worth a rousing acapella *Que Sera Sera.*

Three patients caught it on video before the day was through, as was he.

A copycat air controller in Denver sang it to incoming planes as then did several of his pilots on approach sing it to the less-than-thrilled passengers.

TV advertising began forecasting costs, results, and side-effects with the *'whatever will be will be'* song. *Medicare Advantage* ads began now with a warning that they were being hacked, followed by a hacked *Que Sera Sera* sung by coughing street people (signs said *Medicare Disadvantage*).

Other satirical hacks followed prescription drug ads, and various other hard TV sells direct to consumer. But wait, there was more.

Plumbers on arrival.

Taxis, Uber, Lyft, cruise ships soon had passengers singing the song during any onset.

Contractors and psychiatrists responded by beginning first sessions in kind.

Even marriage counselors in their own first session.

Until that marriage back in Texas where it had all begun.

Two very high-ranking politicians were getting married in a televised ceremony.

In deference to the core beliefs of their party, both groom and bride were packing war weapons.

The minister officiating was somewhat anxious about that and also about the constant coughing in his direction by the proudly unvaccinated guests.

So when it came to his final ministerial words, he simply turned to the television cameras, gestured to the celebrity couple and, shrugging, launched into a chorus of *Que Sera Sera*.

He had only just finished when bride and groom fired simultaneously.

A first for high ratings, the matrimonial couple showing congruency by parallel action. Murder of their minister for the viewing masses.

Their trial was also televised. The judge proceeding by the book.

Except that she had dressed for this television appearance to be as eye-catching as possible, dreaming about her own TV show someday soon.

Other than that she moved the trial ahead with proper judicial procedure.

Until the defense counsel stood and loudly warned the judge on camera that she needed to say to the nation that *this time* she guaranteed a fair trial with a just outcome.

Dared her to promise viewers that result here and now!

Yes, then the judge sang the song.

Honesty in all its candor sat on the bench that day.

The Doctor's Dream

Theme: *Bridey Murphy* Stan Freberg

This really happened. It was my expelled student's dream that especially stood out.

He was in one of the earliest pre-doctoral cohorts at the first freestanding professional school of psychology's San Francisco campus. He was intense, outspoken.

He was also a very bright contrarian. Anything required of him usually led to his immediate rejection. This happened on the first day in my first class with his cohort in their first year of classes.

The initial assignment was to write a paper on advocacy, a core competence on how to make productive change. He objected immediately: *"We're here to learn, not to be forced to write more years of pointless papers. This is a dumb idea!"*

I didn't see much agreement in the other graduate students, most experienced in the field and often older than me. I did see interest in how I would handle this obnoxious challenge. Okay then.

"All right. We are a campus that tries new approaches. You may choose to write this paper instead on why you think it's a dumb assignment."

Laughter in the class.

He agreed. It was a good paper. A fair example of advocacy. Though it was also advocacy for himself. The cohort was satisfied. So was I. The class went well from that point on. It was a few years before I realized I had made a big mistake.

He completed all his academic classes in good order. By his last year in the psychology PhD program he had only to complete a new pre-doctoral internship and his doctoral dissertation.

I was a member of his three-person faculty dissertation committee. In the planning meeting he proposed doing a "theoretical thesis" dissertation which would have been all discussion, something he did well. I insisted he instead gather actual data as evidence for an original idea or contribution to the field. Psychology is primarily an evidence-based science. He balked of course but the other two faculty agreed with me so it was decided. He agreed to comply.

I wasn't his dissertation chair so he worked with another faculty member who had that honor. In a few months his dissertation chair let us know his draft was done and we could schedule an oral defense to complete the process. This defense, reflecting the counter-culture nature of our innovative pioneer psychology school, was this time to be held on a Sausalito houseboat. Not with the full community as happened in later years.

The rules called for us to have at least a month to read and review his draft manuscript. But of course he gave it to us the day before his orals, no apology. I read it that night though I doubt the other two faculty did, given the time squeeze.

The first thing that I noticed was that the numbers in the abstract didn't match the numbers in the text. As Yul Brynner's King of

Siam role made famous on the Broadway stage: it was definitely a *"puzzlement"*.

He showed up in the houseboat, dressed formally, and carrying a bottle of champagne plus four ornate glasses. Clearly he planned for us to all celebrate once the defense was done.

Once he had very briefly summarized his dissertation, I asked the first question. Why didn't the abstract match the text?

He turned red in the face and snapped *"I TOLD you I didn't want to collect any data! So I made the numbers up! Satisfied now?"*

I was not. I refused to sign his approval. He did not pass. The other two faculty tried to mediate, suggesting he might just do a new thesis. At this he rose and walked out of the houseboat. Yes, and he took his champagne bottle and glasses with him.

On arriving at the campus the next day, I learned that he had also been caught forging his internship field placement supervisor's signature on the weekly attendance sheets. In fact the placement had been delayed from opening but he had pretended that he had been going anyway.

So, bright as he was, he had a pattern of cheating. No apology or regret was forthcoming. His position was that he had put in the years, passed his classes, and paid the tuition. What was the problem?

Any of this today would justify immediate expulsion. That was my choice even then. But it required the approval of my own supervisor, the Campus Dean.

A few of the faculty ignored his obvious character disorder and urged that he be given another chance, maybe some psychotherapy first.

The Campus Dean privately agreed with me but wanted me to set up some sort of review panel to mollify the forgiveness faculty. Maybe an equal number of un-conflicted faculty and students. I could chair it without vote.

I met with him. He was sure this would exonerate him and cooperated. We agreed on three specific faculty and three specific students who would be fair to join me as Chair. The review panel commenced its work.

His cheating was confirmed immediately. Yet our panel's weekly meetings on how to respond went on and on for some time.

Of course, the Watergate hearings were being televised at the same time. Seeing our national president being held accountable was national news that continued too. It clearly influenced our local process, although any of the panel's fiercely independent faculty or students at the time would certainly not agree that this was so.

Our president, Nick Cummings, had once asked me who I thought the school's primary client was. Stakeholders like faculty, administration, and staff were not the answer. Nor was it the Board of Trustees or the administration. No, not even the students we were training, the ones we had selected and saw as in our care. Not our financial donors or contributors. Not the accreditation agencies.

No, our primary client for this clinical psychology training school should be the patients our graduates serve, once we grant these new psychologists our doctoral degree. We had an obligation not to graduate any new practitioners that were lacking proficiency, or even ones that could damage the people they treat. First of all, do no harm.

When Nick Cummings first told me this, it made perfect sense. The situation he was addressing at the time was my decision as Faculty Dean to remove an impaired unproductive faculty member, and to hire a competent substitute. There had been a review panel of faculty and students then too, one divided between forgiveness and removal. The primary client was seen by them as either the impaired faculty member or the students that depended on him. That time the review panel was advisory to me. The divided panel chose forgiveness by a single vote, recommending that I retain the faculty member unable to do his job.

I thanked them for their advice, walked the faculty member on a one way trip to the door, said goodbye, and hired a new person who could actually do the job.

Within a month of the arrival of the new high performance faculty member, all of the review board thanked me for my decision, one favoring the students. I told them I had actually decided this in favor of their future patients, the primary clients of the school. People deserving fully trained, highly competent, practitioners.

President Cummings had helpfully clarified this higher priority. Recalling this, it suggested a solution for the current issue with the dissertation student. The Campus Dean liked my idea. Surprisingly, so did the student, confident of his sure and certain triumph.

The idea: I promised him that he could graduate if *all* the faculty and students on the review panel, not including me, would sign a letter affirming that on graduation he would be a competent clinical psychologist, one they would be willing to recommend or refer people to him for his services. He and I signed an agreement for this.

Nobody on the review board would sign the letter endorsing this student as being a competent psychologist. They all cared about our primary client.

Or, as some later said, they cared too about any consequent vicarious legal liability for any of his destructive future actions. He was then expelled with no doctoral degree.

Years later I heard that he, after being expelled without the degree, had claimed he had the degree after all. He tried to practice without it but disappeared when complaints brought in law enforcement.

Forgiveness is wasted on psychopathy.

So that was that. Until a decade later.

I was at a state psychology convention when I spotted the same former student, older now, with a name tag that had *"Dr."* on it.

As we walked toward each other, for a second I wondered if he had matured and forgiveness was actually in order these many years later. Maybe a second chance had worked for him?

When he spotted me, he stopped a few feet away. He scowled. Said: *"Yes, I got this doctorate from a diploma mill, paid a lot for it. All this took me an extra ten years and every second of that was YOUR fault. I dream about killing you by running you over with my car. What do you think about THAT?"*

I just said *"Well, even in your dreams you needed a CAR to do that?"*

He frowned and considered my words.

Psychologist and friend Leland Van den Daele described much of what I say as "time release". This applied here.

I laughed, moved on.

Scent of a Zombie

Themes: *Closer to the Ground* Joy of Cooking; *Bury Me Not* Johnny Cash; *Love Letters in the Sand* Pat Boone

No need to go to impossibly distant planets to find alien lifeforms. They are everywhere here already. Microscopic in a drop of pond water. In a drop of blood. In conditions you would not expect life to thrive- in undersea hydrothermal vents, arctic frozen tundra, arsenic and strychnine poisons. For organized non-human life forms we might pay attention to ants.

Ants can in fact act as individuals. Yet, like bees and wasps, they are still all of them compelled by smell to act in predictable ways. These odiferous commands are called pheromones.

And yes, humans are influenced by some of these scents as well. But not as powerfully as with ants.

When an ant dies, its body emits an *oleic acid* smell. This compels living ants to bury the dead. A process termed *necroptosis* by human observers. Who make the nominal fallacy of assuming that naming something explains it.

No need to explain it to ants. Dead bodies bring disease. They must be parted quickly from the living, buried in the ground as soon as possible.

The dead are a threat to survival and so must be removed once that death smell sounds the alarm.

Some non-empathic human researchers distilled oleic acid into an eye dropper, only to drip it on a very alive ant in a nest. They then watched the live ant being carried to nearby sand, protesting by rapid movements all the way, and buried. Of course it crawled out. The death smell remained and it was buried again. This process continued many times. Finally the zombie ant emerged cleansed of the smell by the sand and was ignored.

Until the researcher laid another oleic drop on it.

Aside from scientific sadism, what applications might this finding generate?

We can speculate.

Billionaires Annual Retreat

Their ritual bathing had included oleic soap and suds. Afterward that night they gathered near a sand dune for a full moon ceremony involving human sacrifice. The location was next to hives of the world's largest wasps.

The sacrifice was more than they had expected.

East Asia

The tiger had killed several children. Then it had been sprayed from a helicopter. National Geographic filmed its repeated exits from burial. Tossed sugar bags to the army ants.

Sand Dunes

They outran a viper but not before spraying it with Oleic. The zombie snake became famous, emerging again and again from the sand around the ant nests. Not happy.

NeoNazi Beach Break in Brazil

Somebody had secretly pre-soaked their bathing suits in oleic acid. Sand ants are relentless.

War in the Jungle

The enemy had entrenched themselves in a leafy cave. Landmines were placed in the path that led to them. Their snipers killed any of us approaching. They had better long range guns. Wait! That useless scientist embedded with us had crawled above their cave. Seems he found a hole and was pouring some smelly stuff in there. Not poison gas- that had been outlawed. He had warned us not to get too close to the cave for another reason. There were large army ants nearby. If they swarmed you, only your skeleton would be left in minutes. Oh! And there they are, trooping en masse into that cave.

KKK Picnic to Remember

The meat had been cooked in a broth that included oleic acid.

And Then

War and picnics. Struck a memory of this time statue:

Afterthought from Psychologist Dr. Gene Orro, WWII Vet. His invited Memorial Day Tribute remarks:

*"As the search for peace remains in vain
The thought of war and heroes gives me pain
So I dare to be so rude
As to wish the ants your picnic food
And pray the clouds obscure our sun with shade
And rain water, cats and dogs, on your parade."*

This was read at his own funeral memorial not long after.

An Edible Easter

Themes: *Proud Mary* Tina Turner; *Go to the River and Pray in O Brother Where Art Thou* Alison Krauss

No, I doubt that the rising of the dead Jesus at what is now celebrated as Easter was the first actual Zombie event.

His body was put in a cave and a huge rock blocked the entrance. But three days later when the rock was moved, his body was gone.

That does not prove he woke up after dying, moved the rock, went outside, returned the rock, and walked into history.

But nobody saw this departure. What if his friends had a secret opening into the cave, removed the body, and left the public to figure it out? This the "stolen body hypothesis". And what might his followers have done with the holy body?

For this likely answer we go the *"Eucharist"* or the *"Holy Communion"* ceremony celebrated for centuries in church by those worshipping Jesus (aka literally the *'son of Zeus'*). A sip of wine and a bite of bread symbolizing the consumption of *"the blood and body of Christ"*.

Did the followers of Jesus actually eat his body and drink his blood? This edible interpretation follows the ongoing church re-enactment.

Easter also involves eating the eggs of chickens, white or multicolored Jackson Pollock style. Early welcome of abortion? Or so the chicken might feel, viewing the consumption of its fetuses. And what of the eating of chocolate rabbits at Easter? Bigoted hate for the carrot chewing species?

Or just delight in recreating the finding of apparently delicious poop in the grass within an actual basket lined with sweet brown confections, and poultry fetuses in a bed of artificial Easter Grass.

How does this tie in to the reputed rise of Christ?

Well, historically, some European cemeteries buried the inhabited coffin with an outside bell hooked to a line in the coffin that might be rung if the body woke up and wanted out.

Today we might see WiFi access.

Perhaps the deceased might also be in a basket-shaped coffin stocked with chocolate rabbits and colored eggs, all on a comfortable sea of Easter Grass.

Happy Easter.

Breaking News

INCIDENTS

Dog travels more than 100 km to bite its owner after being abandoned - junio 17, 2018 Fabiola dog

"A neighbor of New Mexico, Santiago Martinez, went to Albuquerque to spend his holidays like every year. However, this year he decided unfortunately to abandon his cherished dog Golden Retriever, because he explains to some friends «I am sick of the dog because I cannot go to anywhere without having to lug it. At the first gas station, I send him to hell. What he never imagined was that nine days later after many regrets his dog was going to appear right there on the beach, sniffing in each corner in search of its owner. At that moment, Santiago was immersed in a terrible sensation of guilty and he was running to embrace his dog and to reward its loyalty. However, according to witnesses the dog came gasped and it had an expression like: you son of a bitch, you left me in that way, when the dog was in his arms, it didn't hesitate and it bit him hard. Then

Santiago suddenly cried out that they say came to be heard in the Grand Canyon National Park. The dog turned around and went back home making hitchhiking looking like an abandoned dog, so it was adopted by a wonderful family who didn't really know what was going on, while Santiago was getting cured of his wounds at the aid station."

Martin and the Mobile Pork Chop

In the spirit of *this* book, especially in a context of time statues, this will reintroduce two originally dream-initiated chapters from my first published book in 1964: *Uncas Slattery/ The Muddy Chuckle*. New York: Exposition. (1987 version a two-act play.)

Donahue Fix, all three feet of him, rode in to Slattery's Bar & Refuge comfortably on the back of a very large German Shepherd. Patrons flocked around them as he dismounted. Slattery asked Donahue to introduce his mount. That he gladly did, saying his name was "The Lord". "Why?" somebody asked. Donahue shrugged and said "The Lord is my Shepherd."

Science Fiction great Fritz Leiber very kindly read my manuscript before it was published, liked it, and wrote me a quote I could use on the book jacket:

> "The Patrons who assembled daily in Slattery's Bar were, to speak gently, an unconventional, free-wheeling lot. It's unlikely that any saloon, in fiction or reality, has ever been the focal point of activities on quite the same fantastic level as the routine sessions as Slattery's. Presiding over the coterie was Uncas Slattery himself, constantly brandishing

a large piece of black Italian silk for a bar towel and taking a potent interest in the personal affairs and comings and goings of his bar-stool occupants. Among the regulars: the cannibal, whose teeth are filed to sharp points and invariably orders type O blood straight up for refreshment; his little cousin Ira, who wears a Superman suit and is gifted in defying the laws of gravity; the ghoul, bosom friend and formaldehyde with ginger drinking companion of the cannibal; an oversized pet tarantula spider; the prayer-shouting do-gooder Jon Maier, who found it difficult to understand the odd goings-on at Slattery's; Acne Vulgaris, a student who sold pot holders and was smitten by the charms of Mattress Molly; Mrs. Donahue Fix, forever on the warpath and searching for her three-foot husband, who habitually sought and found haven in Slattery's; Uncas' tattooed tramp relative, Uncle Edgar- and other persons of unorthodox leanings. Events took place when these customers drew together in convivial brotherhood or otherwise. No summary can do justice to their flavor or variety. Any reader, however, who has a taste for the off-beat, the far-out, for lampoonery and biting satire on our current mores, manners and morals, will find a delightfully bizarre evening. Mr. Morgan's writing, full of whimsy and the fantastic, has an impromptu touch, the piece de resistance, of a master literary chef who serves a piquant and entirely original mixed salad."

Encouragement gets no better than that.

So I rushed his review to my publisher in New York, along with my manuscript.

Well, these comments by Fritz Leiber appeared fully on the book jacket when it came out in 1964.

But something was missing. The publisher had omitted Fritz's name, crediting his remarks. Nor did Fritz like that a bit either. Sigh.

In college, by the fates, I took a creative writing class, with an instructor, it turned out, that was Fritz's son Justin Leiber.

I did read one of Justin's science fiction books and enjoyed it.

But Justin did not reciprocate. He thought my writing was *"over-opulent"*, gave a B-, and told me to tone it down. The advice didn't take.

Encouraged in another way, and still only in my early twenties, I turned to another celebrated writer, Ray Bradbury.

We had never met but I sent him a guest invitation to my wedding. He responded with a very gracious regrets letter, several beautifully written pages long.

A friendship begun at a distance along with all the other new and unique paths to walk that year.

So here we can offer an optional bonus of two selected chapters from those times for those readers who are curious.

Bless you all.

Martin

Theme: *Moanin* Richard Maltby

DONAHUE Fix sat on the third bar stool from the end with a plump red pillow filling in the gap between stool and the added height that was needed.

"*Slattery!*" he squealed. "*Oh, will you hurry up, man? It's almost time for the little woman to appear again.*"

"*Have some patience, Donahue,*" returned Uncas as he stirred sugar into a tall tumbler of red bubbling liquid.

"*Mr. Fix, pardon me for asking the question, but why do you drink that as you do?*"

Donahue turned to face his questioner, the ghoul, who was waiting patiently for his drinking partner to reappear.

"*I don't see the problem,*" answered Donahue Fix.

"*Let me phrase it this way then. What is Slattery mixing in that tumbler?*"

"*Why a strawberry jello stinger. It is strawberry, isn't it, Uncas?*"

"*Oh, yes. Strawberry for sure,*" it was affirmed.

"*Very well then,*" went on the ghoul. "*Now, whenever I have seen jello made, it was given time to harden. Then it was eaten. With a spoon perhaps. Yes? Yet I can't help but notice that you drink it down on the spot, so here is my concern.*"

"*Morton, you need not be concerned for me, surely!*" replied the little man. "*Save your emotions for those poor souls reduced to eating gelatin in pieces, those poor devils who must digest the gump in misshapen lumps, distorting and twisting the stomach out of its little mind!*"

At this point, Slattery deposited the tumbler before his irate customer. Fix took an immediate sip and then grudgingly dropped four bits into Slattery's palm.

Fix added "*This way the liquid gently fills my stomach and hardens into the very shape around it. It's as comfortable a load as you'll ever carry inside you, and you can bet on that!*"

"*Ohhh!*" answered the ghoul and threw up his hands in amazement.

A shrill bellow filled the air at that instant. "*Donahue!*" It was Mrs. Fix.

Off the stool with a bound, the pillow flying at right angles, and Fix through a low escape hole cut in the wall for that very purpose. Mrs. Fix was beside herself with rage.

"*Slattery!*" she proclaimed. "*I'm coming back here one of these days with an ax. Remember that!*" She was out the front door with a ruffle of injured dignity and a swish of feminine fury.

Uncas, calm in the teeth of times like these, mopped up the counter with his black cloth. Then he turned on the radio. It was a rock 'n 'roll show featuring Ike and Tina Turner, Ray Charles, and the *Bamboushay Steel Band.*

"It's a sad thing that music has come to," commented the ghoul.

"I'm not with you there, Morton," answered Slattery.

"Could you turn it up just the bit?" asked the ghoul.

Soon three or four truck drivers entered to seek respite from the day's troubles. Then Benson Bertotti surrounded by eight B-girls. Then three mailmen, two trolls, and a bus driver. In all the rush and bustle of the hour and all the heart-filled beating of the music, both Slattery and the ghoul forgot about Donahue's tumbler of jello. So it hardened.

And then Mattress Molly, the B-girl, arose in a rage. *"Bar tender, will you please take this glass of whatever the hell it is off the bar?"*

"Certainly, Molly. Has it offended you somehow?"

"It's laughing at me!" she wailed.

"Oh, nonsense," put in the interrupted mailman upon whose lap she had been sitting. He put his ear to the tumbler. *"By golly, Uncas! It is laughing. That's a fact!"*

The radio was unplugged, and the room fell silent. A tiny high-pitched giggle could be heard. Uncas reverently approached the tumbler and looked inside. He motioned the ghoul, who did likewise.

"Did you see it jiggle, Morton?"

"Yes, Uncas. I saw it. You see what has happened, of course."

"*No, I'm afraid not,*" was Slattery's truthful answer. The rest of the customers nodded agreement.

"*Why, it's a simple thing. Life can crop up anywhere at any time. Just take the right rare combination of ingredients at exactly the correct temperature, add a shot of rum, a good bit of the luck, and you have it. You see, the poor thing is obviously alive-living strawberry jello stinger. Ah, well, it might have been worse. It might have been seasoned with bananas.*"

At this last remark the little laugh, momentarily quiet for the ghoul's speech, now doubled in volume.

"*It sure is good-natured,*" remarked Molly. Now that it was apparent the jello had not been laughing at *her,* she felt the greatest compassion for it.

"*Let's give it a name,*" squealed the harpy voice of one of the trolls.

"*A name! A name!*" assented the crowd. And it fell naturally to Slattery's lot to do the naming.

"*How about naming the tad after the newly ordained St. Martin de Porres, the first and only mulatto saint?*" he suggested.

"*I'm for it!*" said the mailman, and the others agreed.

So Martin then it was after that. And Martin became the center of discussion for the rest of the evening. Theories flew back and forth in muddled profusion. Martin himself took an active voice in the discussion until shifted down the bar to be educated by Benson Bertotti and his harem. Before the hour was out a tiny voice of vibrating strawberry jello was reciting back obscenities in Hungarian, Greek, Polish, German, French, Italian, Russian, and Gaelic, not to mention incantations and benedictions, dubious anecdotes, and sharp comebacks. It was quite an education little red Martin was getting.

But even the bizarre grows dull in time. When Lita Tamoshanty broke the bottle of benzine over a sailor's head later that night, all attention shifted to the fracas. From the capsized sailor, the crowd drifted on to other things. A bull gorilla was delivered C.O.D. to Benson Bertotti, which he wrestled then and there, taking two falls out of three. But the poor animal ran amok among the patrons, and there was even more excitement until the cannibal's little cousin Ira, aged three, happened by with his relative and teleported the creature crosstown to the Y.M.C.A. All in all it was a run-of-the-mill Friday night.

At closing time Slattery suggested a toast to their translucent guest. He raised the tumbler for acclaim and ... it was empty.

"*There's been some villainy here!*" he thundered, and all were silent, for Slattery's anger was a rare and unpleasant thing.

"*Whatever's the matter, my good man?*" offered the cannibal in a worried voice.

Slattery's face was the texture of muddy butter and his eyes blazed blue lightning as he slowly announced, "*Someone has eaten Martin!*"

"*Oh, Martin? You called it Martin? I do presume you are referring to that jello in the tumbler?*"

All this the cannibal asked, and it was met with a deep quiet and growing suspicion. "*What do you know of this, Reuben?*" calmly asked Uncas Slattery.

"*Why, I ate him,*" answered the cannibal quite simply. "*I met Donahue Fix hiding in the shrubbery outside,*" the cannibal went on, nervously tugging at the bone in his nose. "*He told me I might finish his jello before it went to waste. So I did.*"

"*But didn't it make any protest?*" asked the ghoul.

"*Some,*" admitted the cannibal.

"*And it didn't bother you any?*" asked a troll, aghast.

"*In my profession you learn to overlook little irrelevancies like that,*" answered the culprit, self-consciously hitching up his horsehair kilt.

"*Ah, well,*" put in Slattery, "*It was legally yours if Donahue Fix gave it to you. He paid for it this afternoon.*"

"*What were his last words, Reuben?*" asked the ghoul, and the crowd began gathering around eager to hear.

The cannibal sipped his formaldehyde and ginger and smiled pointily. "*Why, he just laughed,*" he said. "*He just rippled and laughed.*"

"*I told you he was good-natured,*" said Molly.

"*Aye,*" rumbled Uncas. "*Either that or ticklish.*"

The Mobile Pork Chop

Theme: *"This Little Girl of Mine"* by Herbie Mann
(Alternate: *"Tell the Truth"* by Ray Charles)

Slattery's was a mass of hustling confusion. The humid air of a warm July afternoon crowded against the walls and sluggishly stirred about the open doorway as the Slattery regulars ran in and out with chairs, pastries, costumes, and multicolored paper streamers.

"Benson!" called Slattery, dabbing at his forehead with the ever-present black cloth.

"Yes, Uncas?" Benson Bertotti at full attention was two hundred and eighty pounds of ninety-proof gristle at Slattery's command.

"I want to make sure you know the purpose of these festivities."

"Sure thing, Uncas. That Acne kid and Molly tied the knot today. And we're the reception. See?"

"Very good, lad. Now, seeing as you understand it fully, I am asking you to remember the things you're not to do.

"No fighting. I got that. Eat with knife and fork. Keep my mouth shut when I eat. No leaving my hands on Molly's seat so I can wiggle my fingers when she sits on 'em. Uh ... "

"Yitz?"

"Oh, yeah. I keep Yitz out of sight at all times."

"At all times, Benson. That's important. A ten-pound spider can put a cramp in a wedding reception. Especially on a Thursday."

"Can I feed him under the table?"

"I think that would be all right."

"Thanks, Uncas!"

"All right then, to your post."

Benson back to building a table.

Enter Donahue Fix and wife.

"Mrs. Fix! What a surprise!"

Slattery genuine in his comment here. *"I notice you don't call it a pleasant one,"* Donahue's larger half replied.

"Ah, don't listen to her, Uncas. She's just a little on the embarrassed side today. There's so few people here she knows."

"And the ones I do I wish I didn't," Mrs. Fix went on.

"Well, anyhow, it's a good thing you both could come."

"Do you need any help with the cooking?" asked Mrs. Fix, a bit mollified by Slattery's manner.

"No, thank you. I started out with two chefs this morning, and that turned out to be two too many."

"Who might they be, Uncas?" asked Donahue.

"*Morton and Reuben.*"

"*A cannibal and a ghoul in the same kitchen?*"

"*Yes, if I didn't think I'd rupture their feelings, I'd have heaved them out long ago.*"

"*Feelings!*" Mrs. Fix shuddered at a memory. "*What did you do, Uncas?*"

"*I put Uncle Edgar in charge. He's master of the kitchen now.*"

At that moment Uncle Edgar came to the bar to join his discussers.

"*How are they getting on, Edgar?*"

"*They can't stop the disputing, Donahue. Reuben goes overboard. He has this thing for exotic colors on everything-and Morton goes underboard and insists on more preserves and less spice. But they are doing a fine piece of cooking.*"

"*Like what?*" Here Mrs. Fix posed a question the answer to which she awaited in dread.

"*My dear woman,*" intoned Edgar with true Slattery diplomacy, "*you mustn't spoil the joy that comes to my chefs in the making of their little surprises. Suffice it to say that roasts and vegetables, fruits of all varieties and ancestry, sugared cakes and vintage wines and more have been flowing past my tired old eyes this whole day.*"

I'm sure you'll be pleasantly surprised, Mrs. Fix," said Uncas Slattery.

"*I can imagine,*" she said.

"*This will cost you dearly, won't it, Uncas?*" put in Donahue, a note of worry in his voice.

"Oh, money-" started Uncas.

"Uncas Slattery never liked to think about money. Not as far back as my memory goes. I'm sure every penny he makes off this bar goes right back into his customers one way or another," finished Uncle Edgar with a touch of wistful pride.

Slattery nodded and stepped to the door to help Ira lead in a pig the size of a small cow. Uncle Edgar was appalled.

"I can't work with THAT!" he cried.

Ira gave him a startled look, and the ghoul was instantly out of the kitchen and at the gross oinker's side.

"Not work with it? Not work with it? This is the crowning glory of the whole thing! The high point. And you don't want to work with it!" All this the ghoul said and took a breath for more.

"Now, now," broke in Slattery. *"Uncle Edgar just has a little aversion to killing, is all. You shall certainly have your crowning point, Morton. We have nothing against pork."*

The cannibal put his head out the kitchen door.

"That figures. What do I get to eat then? Old pickles?"

In an hour all the guests were assembled cross-legged around a rectangular table only six inches off the floor. There had not been enough chairs to accommodate the crowd of perhaps a hundred, so they sat on the floor about the massive table space. Each with knife and fork in hand, waiting for the guests of honor to arrive as tantalizing smells rolled out of the kitchen. Then at precisely half past one, Acne Vulgaris and his bride, Molly, walked in upon the crowd.

"Here comes the bride!" sang a hundred majestic voices and not a one in tune. Acne looked deeply hurt. Slattery guessed the cause and started a second chorus.

"Here comes the groom!" sang the crowd and started beating the silverware against the table for their dinner.

But Molly had something to say first, and she pounded her fist against the bar until all eyes were upon her.

"Okay! So we got married. Maybe. But I look at it this way. What's a marriage ceremony if it don't mean something right?"

Silence.

"I said RIGHT?"

"Right!" the crowd obediently echoed.

"Okay," Molly went on. *"So I'd like Uncas Slattery to say a few words just to make it legal. Right?"*

"Right!" they cheered and a clapping ovation followed.

Slattery stood upon the bar with Acne and his bride in blue at his feet and the crowd at their backs.

"Molly, do you love this man?" asked Uncas solemnly.

"I do."

*"Will you always **love** him?"*

"I hope so, Uncas."

"Then will you always be faithful Molly?"

"It isn't likely."

A little laugh started and was stopped by an abrupt wave of the Slattery palm.

"Do you swear to continue being honest with your husband just as you have done this day?"

"I do."

"And do you swear to forgive his trespasses just as you expect him to do for you?"

"I will forgive, Uncas, but won't it hurt anyway?"

"Remember that it does. That's part of the price, Molly. And it cuts both ways, for you or him. Now, do you promise to go your own way if ever your marriage is done?"

"I do."

"Do you, Acne Vulgaris, fully understand this woman?"

"Not a bit, Mr. Slattery."

"I'm pleased to see honesty in you both. Never conceal the truth from anyone you love. I now pronounce you man and wife, and the rest of us. You are married to us all, you two. Remember that, but especially to each other. You may kiss the bride."

Acne got in a quick one on the left side of Molly's lips, but suddenly she was swamped by a pack of well-wishing males claiming their turn. Acne, to his surprise, was carried off to a corner by a female contingent for the very same purpose.

In ten minutes order was restored for dinner, and a luscious dinner it was, including the waitresses. Cannibal held open the kitchen door with pride as they marched out carrying trays of soup and salad. There were twenty of them, all Molly's colleagues, led by Lita Tamoshanty, who put a rhythmic swing to their march as they filtered among the guests. All were nude but for their white napkins converted to bikinis, and their bare skins were painted a deep sea green with Easter-egg dye. Cannibal had this thing with exotic colors.

The soup bowls were divided into thirds and each third contained a different kind of soup-tomato, pea, and chicken noodle. To the side of the bowl was a container of ice for cooling purposes. Next to that was a lever that, when pulled, flushed the leftover porridge into a false bottom out of sight. The salad was ablaze with tomatoes, celery, lettuce, radishes, watermelons, cucumbers, and ten or twelve more varieties of edibles with the smell of Russian dressing in the air.

This was all the cannibal's work, and the color of the soup, ice, salad, and all were a uniform blood red. The food sat before the guests untouched as their hesitation hung thickly upon the air.

The cannibal appeared instantly. *"It's only food coloring. For effect, you know?"* He gave them all a look of earnest appeal.

After a few Irish throats were cleared, the mob dug in. The next course was delivered by the ghoul, smiling and dipping his hat as his ripple soles squeaked in the humid air. Behind him padded five trolls dressed in crepe-paper ballerina costumes with shoes like their leader's. Each carried a silver tray holding preserves of all flavors and a thick loaf of Syrian buttered bread.

Ghoul clapped his hands when the course was distributed, and the help lightly skipped to the kitchen, to return with flasks of golden cider. Glasses were filled. Squeals, then groans and sour looks. The ghoul had aged the cider too long, and it had the taste of vinegar.

Uncas came to the rescue with some casks of vintage wine, and for Reuben, from Morton, delivered by a delegation of five giggling trolls, a ten-pound jar of kosher dill pickles.

Uncle Edgar took command. The green-skinned B-girls brought in the next course, thin slices of roast lamb smelling faintly of rum and seasoned generously with green maraschino cherries. There was applause for Uncle Edgar. After this came helpings of corn and potatoes, all manner of drink, and in the air was the smell of clove incense. Also, a second helping of napkins all around for the waitresses' protection. Even so, there were a few accidents.

"*Reuben, I can't go out there like this!*"

"*Just hold still, female. A little more green dye and nobody will know the difference. And tell those truck jockeys to cease the napkin burning, because there'll be no replacements. Those white stretchees are hard to come by.*"

Uncle Edgar stepped up onto the table and motioned for silence. "*I'm sorry to announce a little delay before the main dish is served. It will give you a chance to relax and build up appetites again, heh?*"

"*How long?*" asked a lumpy voice.

"*A mere three or four hours. Over in a wink of the lids!*"

There was a moan.

"Now, now. It's worth every minute of wait, and I can promise that. Picture a huge pig, ripe and roasted to a tee on the outside but still red and juicy on the inside. It sits stretched before you on the table, and no plates are needed. Just reach forward and cut yourself a fresh slice of pork. In the little wiggler's mouth up front is a watermelon. Now, how about it? Isn't that worth waiting for?"

One hundred raspberries blew an answer.

Since the preliminary courses had been consumed already, it was not too unlikely a task to wait for the main one. Acne and Molly led off with a twist, and in a minute the crowd was doing everything from a rain dance to a ballet in ripple soles.

Five hours went by quickly. The wedded couple received their gifts, piling them behind the bar for later opening. This was at Slattery's instigation, as the majority were empty boxes donated by patrons too poor in funds to give anything else and too rich in the spirit of the thing to go without giving something.

Outside the thunder pounded a steady beat, and lightning crackled across a choking sky. Slattery put an end to the rain dancing and with Benson Bertotti's aid put a canvas tarpaulin over the area where once had been a roof.

Six and a half hours went by. Night was there to stay.

"Uncle, do you realize it's going on nine o'clock?"

"A fine Irish word: o'clock."

"Nevertheless-"

"Yes, Uncas, I know you will be put off no longer. Luckily we are ready."

Slattery reassembled the guests around the table. There were some fresh faces; thirty had gone and forty others had arrived. The green waitresses now sat at places of honor. Putting things to rights were Ira and his formidable parents (the Barbers), one of Morton's prettier ghoul friends (a study in rich blond hair running from eyebrows to incisors), two six-fingered stenographers, one mailman in uniform, and two cops out of uniform (to keep an eye on things until further orders).

At last the swine was carried out upon the table with a plump green watermelon wedged between its jaws. With a cheer, knives rose and fell in a hungry swoop, and flank pieces were sliced off en masse.

"*It certainly is delicious*," mouth-fulled one of the six fingered stenographers to her club mate, a fat piece of dripping pork clutched by the three fingers on her left hand.

Uncle Edgar stood watching the happy group with an excessively thin smile. Meanwhile the cannibal and the ghoul on his either side were looking openly unhappy. Slattery approached the culinary trio without hesitation.

"*What's wrong?*" he asked.

"*Wrong?*" was his uncle's answer.

Slattery thoughtfully tasted a piece of pork cut from a rear flank only seconds before. "*Ummm. Touch of tender in it yet.*"

"*It's been roasting since it walked in the door this morning,*" remarked the cannibal, regardless of Edgar's be-quiet glances.

"*For ten hours?*" cried a surprised Slattery.

"Ah, well, nephew, you know me. Too much heat, and you ruin the meat. Take your time; that's what I say. Let the flesh fall apart when you touch it. Cook it slowly at low heat from the outside in. The only way."

"But ten hours, uncle? How low did you turn the heat?"

"No need to go into technique now. Discuss it later. A little later."

"*Way too few degrees,*" put in the ghoul, his eyes peacefully and innocently aloft under their thick curtain of brow.

Slattery was seized with a vision. "*Morton! Reuben! The truth now. The pig was alive when placed in the oven hours ago?*"

"*That's right,*" they chorused.

"With a tube running from its mouth to the outside for the air that was in it?"

"*'That's right,*" they chorused.

"Otherwise the oven was closed and at ninety-five degrees Fahrenheit, and the pig was quiet because-because Uncle Edgar gave it-"

"*Hold on now!*" cried Edgar horrified.

"*-a bottle of tranquilizers?*" continued Slattery intently.

"*Exactly right,*" chorused the cannibal and the ghoul.

Slattery took a deep breath and shut his eyes.

"*You know how I am about killing anything,*" pleaded Uncle Edgar.

"But what about when the tranquilizers wear off?" asked Uncas in a very, very quiet voice.

"We can take it in the back room after dinner and fatten it up," went on Uncle Edgar. *"Why, we can have pork chops every Sunday and let the animal convalesce all week to grow us more."*

"But what about when the tranquilizers wear off?" Uncas quietly asked once more. But it was too late for an answer.

Mrs. Fix had started a side cut into the watermelon in the pig's mouth. It was one of her sudden unexplainable cravings she will insist on having. Angling for a better cut, she gave the melon a tug. The pig opened its eyes, glared, let out a long grunt, and tugged back. She screamed endlessly.

The swine rose shakily to its feet and hobbled off the table, then out the door to the street with the watermelon in an iron grip between its jaws. Behind it lay a trail of shattered glasses, dripping blood, half-eaten mouthfuls, and screaming patrons.

Acne and Molly alone were oblivious to the noise as they sat looking deep into each other's eyes.

"Thank goodness for that," said Slattery, taking careful note.

Leonard Sly

Theme: *Sweet Dreams* Eurythmics

"We are now faced with the fact that tomorrow is today."
-Martin Luther King Jr.

Joey

Theme: *Rumble* Link Ray

For me, it was always Charles Bronson.

I liked revenge movies as a kid. Especially Bronson's *Death Wish* series. But the absolute best of them was *Chato's Land*!

I know. I know. White guy playing an Indian.

But come on! Half Indian? And he WINS!

Sure. Identification. I wanted to be like Chato. To *BE* Chato.

Got there. Big deal, huh?

I was born Joseph Jimerson, a Seneca child in the Iroquois Confederacy. In western New York state.

Not really as big a deal as I had hoped, less every year while I grew up in public schools.

Stereotypical minority. Few if any whites could really see the actual me, and I was the biggest kid in the class. This all through the grades.

Home was better but had its own heavy, very heavy problems.

I was barely out of high school before I met her.

I was still in the throes of adolescent rebellion against my parents, their restrictions, their tribal biases. Not sure who I was or who I would be, but certain that I was not them.

So about that time I heard the Chippewa were having a celebration.

That was where this Seneca Iroquois would go.

Pain or pleasure, I looked forward to being exactly where I would not be wanted.

Trina

Theme: *These Dreams* Heart

Midnight. And that's when I met her.

She took me away from the crowd, minutes after arriving.

To safety in a grove of trees. Far enough.

Asked why I was so looking for trouble.

Wondered herself why this would matter so much to her. And for a boy from that hostile tribe!

I had no answers. I had no questions.

I kissed her and lost all awareness of anything in this world but her.

Even before I knew it was Trina that I was kissing.

Both of us so impulsive. We knew our families would never approve of this match.

So Trina and I got married as soon as we could, just the two of us there with the official.

And moved into a low rent apartment in the city of Buffalo.

Trina became pregnant immediately.

The next nine months remained the sparkling best time geography of my life.

All my days I would revisit and revisit again that stretch of time and place for strength, for purpose, for joy. For her.

Trina glowed in those days as well.

Pregnancy for her, discomfort or not, was fulfilling.

Each day together was better for us than the last.

We found day jobs but these, relatively pleasant, were just interruptions from the wonderful world we inhabited with each other.

Midnight

Themes: *Walkin' After Midnight* Patsy Kline; *After Midnight* Eric Clapton; *Just a Little Rain* Joan Baez

Some of the tribal friends my age were not about to be left out of this world that I had discovered.

At the least they would throw us a welcome for the baby to come.

Rebellious as me, they talked us into joining them the next full moon in a small city park for this reunion.

That night came in the one month that Buffalo was sure to have great weather. As expected, the July gathering that night was warm, with slight breeze, moon lit fully.

As happens in Buffalo, a distant storm cloud came close enough to begin intense rain.

Everybody ignored it. Eventually it took the hint and departed.

The drums had begun before we got there. Quietly, as the evening was past the time when the white people living around the park would be sleeping. Low and easy like that moment of the weather.

Still, one neighbor heard them.

As she testified later, she had slipped into her robe and slippers, scooted to the park edge, and watched for a moment. Hustled back home. To the phone.

She called the local Fillmore police station. An Indian gathering in the park! Looks like they're about to attack!

Turned out that the night officer thought it a crank call but was bored. So he sent the SWAT team to check it out.

By the time me and my bride arrived, my friends were dead, bodies sprawled everywhere.

Reporters had begun arriving so the Swatters just arrested us alive, took us to the Fillmore station. Placed us in separate holding cells for the night.

The Crime

Themes: *You Got to Run (Spirit of The Wind)* Buffy Sainte-Marie & Tanya Tagaq; *Topsy part two* Cozy Cole; *Custer Don't Ride Good Any More* Buffy Sainte-Marie & Johnny Cash

No telephone call allowed. Reporters gone.

My lone guard was a white man that called himself *"Tojo"*. I kept asking after my wife, asked for a call, a lawyer. Tojo just increasingly annoyed by these interruptions to his nap.

Tojo ignored me for a time, until he finally strode up to my holding cell, brandishing what looked like a samurai sword. Through clenched teeth, trying to look like a Clint Eastwood samurai, Tojo explained it was the real thing, very expensive, deadly sharp. His affectation, his obsession.

He said that he was hoping I would break out somehow so he could slice and dice me with the sword. Did some slash motion with it. Well, pretty fast actually. Impressive.

I ignored him as best I could. Mourned my friends as their deaths set in.

Suppressed my anger until I knew what I could do about it all.

Increasingly stressed about my wife's safety. Trina!

Kept asking Tojo.

An hour later in his quiet but annoying evening, Tojo unlocked my cell door. Said: *"Oh! Look what I have done now! Well, I'll just wait back in my desk. Hope you don't make a run for it."*

I thought this pretty hokey. Badly scripted movie. So I lay down on the bunk and ignored the unlocked cell door. Ignored Tojo and his damn sword.

Waited as patiently as I could for the sunrise and a new shift.

Worried about my pregnant wife. She was in another remote part of the cells, too far away for her to hear me or for me to hear her.

Another hour passed.

Then, I heard Trina scream. Not possible but I heard it in that second as though she was in my cell. Heard fright, pain, and then mostly rage. Suddenly silence.

Enough!

The adrenalin rushed through my body, my heart rate magnified, time stopped. Then time expanded but only to a split second.

I'm out the cell door. Tojo at me with the sword.

He was fast but not fast enough.

Tojo flying from my push, hard against a wall. Wall pushing sword into his chest.

Me grabbing the sword, pulling it out to me, through the doorway, racing the path that the scream came from.

Found her holding cell. Stopped for a split second to take in the tableau.

She was face down on the bed, naked, passed out.

On each side of her was a male guard, holding her up on her knees while the third officer, wearing an open white coat (a doctor?), had his back to the doorway and was doing something to her. There was blood around her head.

As I moved closer, faster than time, there was no motion in this tableau. I could now see that the guards on either side of her wore no pants and were aroused. I could see that Trina's water had broken and was pooling below her, mixed with blood. And then I could see that the white coated man was also without pants and had entered her rectum.

My sword took off the heads of the guards on either side of her, then it separated the white coated man from that portion of himself that he had inserted into my unconscious bride in front of him. Somehow, he was able to realize this in that time fraction before he lost his head as well.

I threw the sword full strength into the room wall where it remained up to its hilt.

Still accelerated, I put on the white coat, wrapped my still breathing Trina in the blanket she was on, and carried her outside to the street. To the ambulance parked nearby.

That police station was known as the *"Bloody Fillmore Station"*. Ambulances were called there so often in the night that the company eventually stationed one there on a regular basis.

Cut commute time and gas costs.

I woke the two men napping in there and in a minute they were all racing with us to the hospital emergency room.

The Bond

Themes: *Crying* Roy Orbison & KD Lang; *Riders on the Storm instrumental only* Doors; *Side by Side* Kay Starr

I was there when my son was born. His mother was dead.

Till death do us part had come way too soon.

I prayed goodbye to my love, my Trina.

I expected that I would be dead too, any minute now.

My son born the next of kin.

Yet. I held him in my arms, touched my lips to his forehead. Felt his awareness somehow. Connected to him. Promised that I would still take care of him somehow. Not possible but the words came out and I knew it was the truth.

The delivering doctor stepped out into the hall, came right back.

Said to me *"The police out there don't want to shoot all of us in here just to get to you. They say you must surrender immediately and that won't happen."*

I knew that once I stepped out, they would shoot me anyway.

Just then it all caught up to me. I handed my son to the doctor. Let my exhausted body collapse to the floor. No more memory.

I woke many weeks later in intensive care.

My legs and arms were in casts. My chest was wrapped heavily in bandages. My face itched, maybe stitches. I was hooked up to an IV drip and many instruments. I couldn't speak as my throat had something embedded into it doing my breathing. Ironically, despite all this, I was chained to the bed. So I went back to sleep for another week.

Eventually I reeled back my memory to find out how all this breakage had happened to me back while I was first passed out.

I had always been fascinated by hypnosis and was a natural at it. With that, I was able to reach that one time, felt the kicks and breaks. Oh. The police that arrested him after I collapsed in the emergency room. I heard a voice then say *"Don't kill him yet! Smash what you want but the families of his victims, our brothers, have the right to see him die for what he done, be there when it happens."*

I had a decent lawyer for the trial. Reporters and television were there.

I pled guilty as that was not in dispute. I had not intended to kill Tojo as that was self-defense. I *had* intended to kill the three that were assaulting and killing my pregnant wife as her birthing began. In fact I testified that I relished the memory, wished I could do it again. No remorse.

The prosecution pointed out that I had killed four officers, one a doctor, three by beheading. Said I was a grave danger to the community. Should get the death penalty. While the families of my victims watched.

The judge pondered these arguments as well as the TV ratings. I had become a hero to some while a terrifying threat to others. The grisly deaths of four officers had to be punished.

Clearly though my murders were not premeditated. Plus there was that media frenzy about the doctor's penis being found in the rectum of the dead woman.

The judge finally announced that Joseph Jameson would serve four consecutive life sentences, one for each victim, with no parole. But no execution, given the, ah hum, extenuating circumstances.

So a life in a cell.

The defense lawyer pointed out to the judge, also the media, that the police would still have the guards kill me in prison, soon as I arrived.

So I got a solitary cell in a maximum security prison.

My home now and always.

The prisoners there with seniority or connections ran that prison. They kind of appreciated what I had done and why.

So I got a large cell with perks. A small connected high-walled exercise room with a sky view- access an hour a day. I settled in. To my tiny new universe.

In my mind I heard Trina share this with me: Audra McDonald's *My man's gone now* from Porgy and Bess.

Leonard: Next of Kin

Theme: *The Wayward Wind* Tex Ritter

Just like the song, my favorite eventually, I was born the next of kin.

My mother died on the delivery table. My father was only beginning his four consecutive life sentences in maximum security and was clearly out of the picture.

So while the hospital social worker tried to reach my deceased mother's married sister, far away, I had lived and needed a name.

The social worker just said to name me temporarily with my mother's last name: Jimerson. Her married name. Her husband's name. She said that once the aunt and uncle can come and get me, they could do the actual naming.

If they decided to keep me.

Hard to know, she said, what these Indian people will do. Joked about maybe a rotisserie?

I didn't laugh.

DREAMS AND TIME STATUES

Leonard: Aunt Rhoda and Uncle Manny

Themes: *Heartbreak Hotel* Link Ray; *Half Breed* Cher

My aunt and uncle took me home.

At first, my mother's sister focused on mourning her loss. But soon Rhoda was mothering the baby, me, as it was needed. Her husband joined in this, happy to have a boy to raise already. They hadn't been married long enough for bringing their own into the world.

But Rhoda had ongoing nightmares. She knew my father was gone for his lifetime and then some, but in the dream he came for his baby, killed her and her husband.

Then she had dreams that showed the baby growing into somebody just like his scary Seneca father. Bound to look like him. She seemed to feel my father's presence embedded in the baby, in the boy. She wanted to mother the child with love but this invisible paternity presence scared her.

Finally, she told her husband that she was afraid her fears would hurt their boy. Said Manny should take over fully. Raise him to be Chippewa, to follow the Ojibway path.

Manny complied with good will. He had no nightmares about my Iroquois father. That man was as good as dead. He no longer existed for any tribe nor did he deserve to.

But what to name his boy?

Manny thought on this for a day, slept on it for a night.

He had a way with dreams. He would ask his dream self a question as he dozed off at night. On waking, an answer would be ready. For which he gave thanks each time.

The answer for baby Jimerson was easy.

His boy would choose his own name when he was ready. All children reach a young age when they seek an adult identity. If it is not thrust upon them by others. Manny would help his boy think for himself and choose who he will become. My uncle was certain that his boy would not choose to be his father. Nor would he be expected to be a copy of his uncle or aunt.

Yes. Good path.

But for then, his boy had only a last name. Well. He'd borrow the first part of it and call him 'Jim'. Time to change Jim's diapers, then feeding. Then someday he would get around to tell his new son about the name choosing.

Manny was surprised at how much he liked doing this. At least for me. I think I understood I was safe with him. As to what he had decided about my name, no argument about any of it. Ever.

Leonard: Lake Erie

Theme: *Time After Time* Samantha Crain; *Sing Our Own Song* Buffy Sainte-Marie

My uncle and aunt lived by the great lake named Erie. It was beautiful there, even in the fierce winters or seemingly endless snow storms, towering drifts.

As I grew, I learned from Manny about my parents.

My mother had grown up in a Chippewa enclave. Manny and Rhonda were from there too. But my mother had met an Iroquois man from the Seneca tribe and loved him.

Nobody had approved of this match in either culture. Such disapproval for young adults can be sufficient grounds for marriage. And so, for them, it was.

Historically, the Iroquois was a confederacy of six tribes, mostly settled around the Great Lakes. Later, the Ojibway joined into their own rival confederacy with two other smaller tribes and moved into the same lake territory as the Iroquois. Peaceful at first but not for long.

Ojibway led their confederacy against the Iroquois in what the history, written often by French and British colonialists, also competing with each other, called this contention between the two tribal confederacies a war.

The Ojibway confederacy, known as Chippewa, prevailed. Settled by Lakes Erie and Huron. The Iroquois moved farther east and south, while the Chippewa moved west, to other larger Great Lakes.

My father was Iroquois. Officially Seneca, but Manny said he was also descended from a white woman named Mary Jameson who became famous writing about growing up Iroquois. Hence the name Jimerson, somewhat changed in spelling over the years.

Manny also took care to share the good things about my father's people. Including how the Iroquois confederation had influenced Jefferson and Franklin in writing the American Constitution plus the foundations of a viable democracy. Not easy holding six tribes together much less than 13 colonial tribes of European immigrants.

My father had already given me this history at night but he was pleased that Manny did also. The First Nations helped create our present USA nation. Mixed feelings from my dad about how wise that was.

Back to Rhoda and Manny's family history.

They stayed where their families had lived for generations, by the great Lake Erie. Moving nowhere else but in an ever smaller group.

In time, their lake was being overwhelmingly polluted by growing industry. You could see reddish dust coming from the steel mills and settling into the Great Lake. Newspapers called it innocent red algae. A fire in the lake's center kept burning. And, a major component now in the lake was strychnine poison.

Manny said it was a sign they were no longer welcome.

Headlines nationally announced the death of Lake Erie. Said no life survived there. I knew better.

As a little boy I liked to play in the fields near the lake. Some small streams were in a runoff, as full of poison as the lake it had come from. There, the day the newspapers said no life had survived, I caught a tadpole swimming along just fine. Brought it home.

Put it in a big glass fishbowl with two large snails and no fish. Keep them company.

Looking carefully at this resident tadpole, I worried that the two bigger snails might eat it. Not a problem it turned out.

By day two, the tadpole was twice as large while the snails were floating, empty shells. Looking closer, I saw that the tadpole had teeth.

Waved goodbye as I flushed the killer down the toilet.

Later wondered what it would turn into as a frog.

Such extremophiles are creatures that can survive anywhere they are not supposed to.

I thought of myself that way when my aunt and uncle said we were all moving to the city of Buffalo.

Leonard: Leonard Sly

Themes: *Tumbling Tumbleweeds/Don't Fence Me in* Sons of the Pioneers with Roy Rogers and Trigger (From the *Hollywood Canteen* movie *Happy Trails*).

I liked Roy Rogers a lot. All through the early grades I carried a lunch pail to school with his picture on it. I loved the way he handled horses and tricks with them.

I sang his songs at home, maybe with a few changes ("*Happy Trails to you, until we eat again..*")

Even Uncle Manny agreed he was the best movie cowboy out there, though he wished he was more on the Indian side. Then Manny's wish came true.

We all watched the weekly TV show *"This is Your Life"*. Host Ralph Edwards would surprise an audience guest with a live biography. And one time, while we watched, the surprised guest turned out to be Roy Rogers! For real! ONLY his name turned out to *not* be Roy Rogers. No, it was *"Leonard Slye"*. AND, on his mother's side were Choctaw ancestors. Too good to be true but the *King of Cowboys* was an *Indian*!

Well, long after the show, this was always played down by his promoters. Neither he nor his mother were registered in the Choctaw Nation. Well, yes, he did have kind of an Indian face (at one time work was done on his eyes to change this and make them rounder but fans objected). None of this mattered to me or my family.

In fact, that's when I took on my real name. From then on I would be *"Leonard Slye."*

That night my secret visiting father gave his conditional blessing. The condition: drop the *"e"* in *"Slye"*. Just to be clear that you can be named after somebody you admire but save room to be yourself. He quoted some guy named Oscar Wilde *'Be yourself. Everyone else is already taken."*

Manny and Rhoda were okay with my choice and my brother thought it was cool. So *Leonard Sly* it was. Goodbye "Jim" Jameson.

My classmates were now too old for those Cowboys and Indian games but they still needed some reminding every time they came up on my name that I was *both*.

Like Roy.

Joey: Ghost Walker

Themes: *Chain Gang* Oscar Brown Jr.; *I'll Never be Free* Kay Starr & Tennessee Ernie Ford; *I am A Man of Constant Sorrow (with Band)* Soggy Bottom Boys

Time on my hands. Years.

One of my perks was library privileges.

Not in person but I could request books and they would come.

Read the classics. Improved my vocabulary.

Learned so many new things, present and past, about the outside world.

I continued my readings in hypnosis, parapsychology, and then in the Robert Monroe trilogy of Out-of-Body or OBE experiences.

I got very good at this psychic and OBE stuff.

I also realized that I could use this to keep my promise to my newborn son.

I would watch. I would be in his head when invited or needed as an advisory whisper.

I would spend my incarcerated days with valuable work.

Caring for my son. Being a father.

Decades passed.

Joey: Library Scrap Book

Themes: *Magic Man* Heart; *Tall in the Saddle* KD Lang

The cons running the prison library still keep me in great supply with books and video.

I spend hours daily consuming these. Plus the martial arts and exercises. And somehow, my son absorbs all of this, maybe in his sleep.

Fair enough because I wake up with whatever he learned in his classes that day.

Now you might think the grades through high school would have little to teach me as an adult. But how many pieces I missed!

Now I have it all.

Even the straight-A kids get by with, say, 90%+ retention. But that means they miss 10% of everything every year- it *accumulates*!

Not for me and Leonard. We share it all.

Special fun getting our full national and tribal history. Lots missed there the first time.

Leonard: My Secret Twin

Themes: *Every breath you take* The Police; *Rainmaker* Strunz and Farah

Through my earliest years he taught me all that school never did.

He was there to explain life, what to do in a crisis, what words meant.

Then, by the time I was in college, it was an even exchange.

My courses were all audited by my father. He of course learned faster than I did. Nor would he ever give me the answer on a test.

Said the best learning would be when I figured it out for myself. Or, even, made mistakes I could learn from. Like he had learned from his bigger ones.

After I graduated I traveled. Many countries, especially indigenous Nations within Nations. Tapestry of cultures. Joey traveling with me as a special guest.

Leonard: The Audit

Theme: *The Great Pretender* Platters

Joey had, over the years, enhanced his sense of humor. It kept madness away.

In the beginning he focused on the flexibility of language. To prepare me for my tax audit, he shared this insight: *"Your audit will be face-to-face with a tax employee whose job depends on squeezing as much money from you as he can. Truth is not the issue. But for perspective, know that historically thousands of taxpayer victims were marched into a huge room with very high ceilings and robbed en masse by the auditor. In time that very room was soon called an 'auditorium'."*

Joey loved the language twists, especially the colorful complaints and curses.

Like the friendly Irish insults: *"Stinkarooney"* and *"pogue muh ho-in"* (kiss my ass) or *"Pug Mahone's"* (a restaurant in Billings, Montana). Or the Polish for 'up yours' *"Yupsha Hooya"*. The more common Polish curse was "Shokref" (aka Dog's Blood). Coptics in Egypt dismissed verbal attacks with *"Let the dogs bark."* In Hawaii, a Korean ethnic complaint about trouble was called being in *"Deep Kimchi"* or, similarly, the disrespectful *"Up the Yin Yang"*. And the Sicilian verbal challenge a friend of mine was convinced that was an off-menu festival Chinese dish, dating back to Marco Polo, to insist upon ordering it in an Italian restaurant: *"Ba Fun Goo"* (Go screw yourself)

Joey's favorite was when a young Burt Reynolds was introduced to Marlon Brando as *"the next Brando"*. Marlon just sneered and turned his back on Burt. Burt, when asked about this, said he was so angry that he wanted to *"punch Brando so hard his ancestors would hurt."*

Joey's sense of humor even made it to my answering machine in my own first apartment.

At his request, the message was answered by a random rotation of famous voices: James Earl Jones, Wanda Sykes, Morgan Freeman, Buffy Sainte-Marie, Adele, Daffy Duck, Porky Pig, and Bugs Bunny. When it was their turn, each would say: *"Holy Doughnuts! Now with Wafer and Chaser!"* And then, also randomly, the message would be replaced by a segment of Screamin' Jay Hawkins singing *Constipation Blues*.

My phone got so popular I rarely was able to use it.

Yes, as far back as I can remember, Joey was in my head, part of me. At first, all the time. Then, in the grades, he was just there when I wanted him to be, invited, or in a crisis. Once I was an adult he felt like a normal part of my thoughts.

He told me that he was a separate person, my father, but his body was stuck in a place where he could not leave.

He did need his sleep and sometimes his privacy. So invitations became mutual.

In my teens I wanted my own privacy. He respected that.

But he was always there when I needed him. Seemed to grow smarter, wiser, as I got older.

Sure, he is my father, ever separated in body.

Time passing as I became an adult, we shared so much experience that we grew to think of each other much like twins.

Though he was always clear that he was my father with a mind of his own.

I'm a son, so me too.

Naturally some arguments.

He was right about this one.

Leonard: No Sexcuses

Themes: *Great Balls of Fire* Jerry Lee Lewis; *Spill the Wine* Eric Burdon & War; *Slapping Medicine Man* 1491s

When I was 21 I was finished with college.

Graduate school would be later.

I got to know a lot of women.

Joey stayed out of this pretty much at first.

Said I had to learn from my own mistakes.

Leonard: Dream Trauma

Theme: *Dream Weaver* Gary Wright

But he would help me with any dream trauma from those mistakes.

Joey had plenty of his own trauma to work with.

To do this, he studied David Cheek's hypnosis reframing and *Senoi* nightmare resolution methods.

He even mastered, remotely from his cell, Robert Monroe's transit levels for lucid dreaming. Out-of-body or OBEs he had already been doing with me, at least internally.

At the highest Monroe level, where most reaching there made contact with a higher form of life or divinity, Joey just roared with laughter. The first such release in years. He realized he had been suppressing joy throughout his post-Trina ordeals.

Joey considered this joyful tsunami the finish line of successful healing.

As much as that can happen with such overwhelming loss.

As to the *Senoi* method, instead of turning threat into alliance, he would stand in for any tiger or giant by being there himself, flowing through the nightmare with me. Though only by my invitation. And very rarely interrupting in any way.

Hear is the method he used with me:

1. Lie down in bed, lights out except for a night light high up but in my view.
2. Focus on the beginning of a relationship I want to forget. See her face.
3. Now sleep. (I was taught by Joey to do this easily).
4. I see my dream, including the trauma, but from a distance as in a movie theater.
5. I am to be aware of feelings throughout, mine and hers, as another dimension of the experience.
6. I am also to be aware of anything I do in the dream to make things better. These successes are essential answers to the question *"What are you going to do about it?"* (Joey sometimes says *"What are WE going to do about it"* Sometimes. Rarely.)
7. Joey remains a silent observer but there if needed.
8. At the close of the dream I wake and write it all down.
9. As I do so I am to continue to be aware of the emotional dimensions of the story as well as any good responses to the situation.
10. When I'm done writing I can still imagine and reframing in which I imagine, knowing what I know now, how I could have made it better. This I keep.

I had only to write down the traumatic dreams and they lost their hold on me.

In the generation younger than me, cursive (love the name) writing is a lost art. Seen as obsolete and unhelpful.

They only push keyboard buttons on their phone to text squeezed tiny messages.

Or even just use the app that turns their voice into print and sends it anywhere they like. And, by mistake, anywhere they don't like.

But Joey insisted on me learning this direct handwriting method.

Told me when I was young that it was a secret code. Even had me write letters to send by postal snail mail.

And here it helped. Writing out the dreams helped heal any damaged emotions.

It gave me a careful distance, allowing understanding, release, even laughter.

Joey liked this too.

Wanted to hitchhike to as many of these varied relationships as I would let him.

Leonard Dreaming: An Erotic Trilogy

Theme: *IN A GADDA DA VIDA* Bart Simpson version

Joey was sure that his techniques were sound and I agreed. But I was ready for something much more positive than trauma. This dream did not need Joey's help. Clearly a sign I was okay, at least for this night.

My dream:

An unforgettable summer day. Just a priest in the sunshine, collar intact.

I sat on the park bench outside my apartment, one facing my front door. In my mind I was listening to the Audra McDonald version of *Summertime*.

She sat down next to me. A nun but in comfortable outdoor clothes.

Wedding ring to Jesus on her hand.

She smiled at me. Said *"I love the Audra version best too."*

What? Mind reading?

I took a fresh look at her. There was a colorful haze around her.

I said *"There's a golden glow about you. Somehow deep blue lining at the edges."*

She looked startled, then pleased.

"Nobody has ever seen my aura before, just me. Do you do this all the time?"

"Never. Don't even see my own, if I have one."

"You do! Blue like mine but a golden red flame at the center. And, oh, growing."

"I see the same thing in you! Growing."

She took my hand. I did not pull away.

But tried to calm down. Said: *"My friends after the service were bragging about their devotion to the church, kind of 'holier than thou'. For my turn I just shrugged and said 'As to me, I've been devoted since birth. How? Because my mother was a nun and my father a priest.' They were not impressed."*

"Was that true?"

"No, but it has happened to others. Sometimes it works out very well. Though of course they need the return to civilian life. Can't continue as priests and nuns. Not allowed to marry and still serve, at least so far. Got my eye on Pope Francis though."

Her glow, an aura she calls it, was glowing a warm flame now, red gold like she said I have. Hers was enveloping me too now, the both of us.

She asked *"Do you agree that a nun and a priest be happily married then?"*

I answered immediately *"I do."*

She mused a moment.

Then *"I do too. Marriage happens when a couple declares before God that they will share all their life in love. No ceremony beyond that really needed. Do you agree?"*

I was distracted by our intersected flames, and my body becoming more aroused by the desire of the moment. We were on fire.

I did my best to ignore this, sent the erotic energy to the sky, as much as I could, not much. Suddenly we knew each other's thoughts, life to that point.

Then answered her question simply: *"I do."*

"Well! I do too! We have said this 'I do' twice now. If we say it again, we, I believe, will be married!"

We both laughed.

I added *"We haven't even said our own names yet. Important? No? Okay, that will come."*

I put on a fake serious face and said a firm *"I do!"*

And suddenly realized I deeply meant it.

She took a breath, looked to the heavens, and said *"I do!"* as well.

Then she kissed me. We both did. Time stopped for a little while.

Nor had we noticed it was raining. With the sun still out.

We ran to my front door. Entered the little room with the bench and places to put our shoes before going into the apartment.

We took off more than our shoes. Quickly. My clothes in a reasonably folded pile. Hers scattered like leaves. I right away liked her system better.

We somehow got to my bed in time. Intense. Delicious. Overwhelming.

I still couldn't see her aura, or my own, but I could feel their warmth. We remained merged, even during breaks.

Seems it is more than sex. I knew it would last a lifetime.

I suppose we had lost count but maybe at least an hour or two had gone by before we stopped to catch a breath.

I spoke first: *"This is marriage then?"*

"Yes. Though I think we just had the beginning of our wedding night."

"The beginning? Great! To continue.."

And yet, sigh, I had another question: *"You still wear your wedding ring to Jesus. Even if we no longer be priests or nuns, are you still his wife?"*

"Of course. That vow is as sacred as the one we just took."

"I don't understand."

"True, we can't stay in the church as we have. But it is also sacred to be married and have a family. As to Jesus, he is very polygamous, having so many legions of my sisters wearing his wedding ring. Further, he belongs to the Holy Trinity of Father, Son, and Holy Spirit. Clearly he approves of threesomes."

I had no time to consider this wonderful interpretation as once again our bodies merged. I still didn't know her name.

-

And her face in the dream was the face of the woman I call my *"Keeper".*

Leonard: A Rose by Another Name

Added Themes here: *Love Rollercoaster* Ohio Players; *The Good, the Bad, and the Ugly* Danish National Symphony Orchestra; *Trail of Broken Hearts* KD Lang; *Slide Guitar Blues* (any)

Making Joey laugh was easier now, yet still something I liked to do as much as time and imagination allowed. He for ears had little to smile about in his prison universe.

Knowing how interested he was in names and rebellion, I did amuse him much once when I subbed for a friend in a high school history class. My friend was to have lectured these teenagers about Henry Ford and other originators of successful corporations. The point was to get them excited about the mythic heroes of capitalism.

Of course, Henry was notoriously grumpy, especially in his anti-Semitic and fascist rants. Further, I had read his assembly line innovation was really his wife's idea. So, in class, I began with this other perspective on Henry as a hero, not denying that his company was a success right into the present.

But then, momentum led me to have fun (Joey was watching) as follows:

-The *Chrysler* car company was founded by Jesus Chrysler.

-The third of the big three auto companies in our country was founded by a war deserter, an officer named General Motors.

-The successful fast food company of *Jack-in-the-Box* was founded by an undocumented immigrant named Cosmo Jackov. He originally named his company after himself but *Jackov-in-the-Box* was shortened to lose the "ov" by his embarrassed wife.

Given that my post-Ford history was all bogus, I was never invited back.

Though as that generation of children aged into the adult population, rumors may have arisen.

Joey was delighted. Made him happy for a while.

He had been studying Latin in his ongoing progress to raise up his imprisoned body and mind.

Not to mention his unique sense of humor.

Used Latin somewhat modified to swear with.

A favorite was modifying the *Peace Go with You* blessing to *Pox Vobiscum* or *Pox Go with You.*

Joey was with me, when invited, through most of my 20 years of dating.

His encouraging Latin phrase for this was an altered Julius Caesar phrase: *Veni Vidi Vici* to *Vidi Vici Veni* or *I Saw I Conquered I Came.*

He also delighted in renaming these women for me as the spirit moved him.

From the book *Time Statues Harvest,* to provide me with caution regularly, this next was his favorite page on dating:

**A rose by any other name
Won't know the difference**

And neither will they

So Joey's sense of humor and, I suppose, paternal wisdom, kept the naming of my dates ongoing.

These are the ones I wrote down: Abundance, Angelic Nurse, Auckland Madam, Bahfun Goo, Bovina LaVache, Cassandra Keester, Clandestina, Cinderella La Pumpkin, Compassionata, Copra Lite, Crab Cakes, Drisophila Melanogaster, Dulce Cagada, Durian Dufus, Fellatia Listerini, Fresno Astrologia, Fur, Karen Clock Blocker, Lena the Gangster, Lotta ("Lottie") Skank, Madame Aukland, Maggie Bolus, Medea Manners, Mia Hooha, Pinky Pomeroy, Porcina, Rump Patter, Sandbox Belva, Shaitania, Urea ("Rea") Drumpf, Vanity Blemish, Yupsha Hooya, and, finally, maybe a happy exception, *The Keeper*.

He was harder to please than I was by far. But he was usually right.

Each one had her own story over the years.

The Keeper is the only happier story. Just beginning. To be told another time as her life with mine progresses.

Still. Many thanks to the ones that made both her and me really happy for at least a little while. Like Oblivia.

For the rest, my sense of humor was fully tested.

Maybe theirs too, for those that had one.

Leonard: Joey had some advice

Theme: *Spinning Wheel* Blood, Sweat, and Tears

Joey said he had found tagging along to my dreams, when I let him, fascinating.

Thanked me for bringing him back into my private life.

He had listened to all of it and helped when invited. Just hadn't been invited yet.

Laughed, saying *"Still, every time in waking life you fell, you landed higher."*

Finally Joey just said: *"Stop looking. The right woman will find you. You might come across each other by accident. You'll both know."*

I was not convinced.

So Joey added *"Already happened for me."*

In jail?

Joey: The Keeper

Theme: *Night Must Fall* Miriam Makeba

Leonard is very private about this *"Keeper"*.

I tell him that when I was a kid, we played marbles. The *"keeper"* was one so beautiful and unique that you never let go of it. Of course, if we call a woman your *"keeper"*, does that mean she is your property, much like a great marble?

Leonard says no, emphatically. *"Sure she's beautiful and unique, body and spirit. But she's nobody's property. Free as the wind. Along with me, she is the keeper of our dream. To fully share our life together. We've just begun."*

Leonard is in his forties now. He was always smart but now he's matured and has wisdom, insight into other humans that cross his path. After so many false starts and star-crossed adventures, he may well have found his soulmate. I feel his excitement, his joy.

I look forward to meeting her somehow, at least in his mind. But, for now, he just says *"in time"*.

For that matter, his timing is excellent. He needs to let me go.

We have trimmed back our being together for some months now. We just check-in once a week, except for a crisis or projects. He's getting ready to move on. To this Keeper.

And that's just right for my phase of life too.

My excitement is building. I know this means a powerful change is coming.

I don't know why but this makes me really happy.

In my own dream, I see that all my years of bring imprisoned in this box are about to come to an end.

Even if that means my exit in a box.

Leonard: Joey's death

Theme: *Riders on the Storm instrumental* Doors; *My Man is Gone in Porgy & Bess,* Audra McDonald

I got the call late that night.

As the sole family contact they regretted to inform me that Joey was found dead in his cell.

No, no need for you to come here.

His body was taken by the jail physician for an autopsy and burial.

All done.

Again, regrets.

Joey: Storm's Sanctuary

Themes: *Stormy Weather* Kay Starr; *I'll Fly Away* in *O Brother where Art Thou* Allison Kraus; *Ghost Riders in the Sky* Willie Nelson & Johnny Cash;

I woke into darkness. Huge hands covered my eyes and, yes, most of my left and right face too. I was lying on what felt like an iron chair. No. Raised a little upright on some kind of hospital bed. Each of my hands tied to a side, as were my feet. Tied with? Rawhide? Not rope.

I was still tired.

Sensed no immediate menace from the hands. Friendly darkness.

So I used this opportunity to get more sleep. Out like a light.

Waking sometime later. Into a dimly lit cavernous room.

Well, awakened actually by the owner of the hands.

The hands were gone from my eyes.

Seeing that they were connected to an arm and a body of a very large frowning Indian man.

DREAMS AND TIME STATUES

"He's awake now. Should I cover his eyes again?"

"No, it's okay. He can see me now. Before he goes back to sleep again!"

I looked straight ahead at an apparent vision. A woman beautiful in an elegant way, looking young but with flowing white hair, dressed in black- a judge's robes?

She seemed very close in front of me. No. She's actually at the far end of the room. She is just huge, larger than the hands guy. Almost my size.

I'm in a massive room with walls made of embedded rocks.

The light is low but adequate even though I can't see any source.

She spoke.

It is not a young voice, strong, a female version of James Earl Jones. Seemed to come at me from all sides.

"Welcome to the waking world Ghost Walker. Please stay here long enough for us to talk. You, I'm sure, will want to know where you are and why. Your questions will be answered. Try me."

"How long was I asleep?"

"Surprising first question. About two days. Not counting this last hour. Next question?"

"His hands sure helped me snooze. Stick around big guy." (Large standing man snorts.)

"All right. My name is Joey, not umm, 'Ghost Walker'. Who are you guys?"

"Introductions? Fair enough. He is my grandnephew. You may call him Roger. He brought you here. Thank him later and often. Here I am called Storm."

"As in Marvel? Do you control the weather?"

Roger spoke for the first time. Powerful sound but somehow friendly like Morgan Freeman's voice

"She doesn't control the weather. She IS the weather."

"Thank you Roger. That will be your last cliché for the evening. I'm not the Marvel version of Storm. But growing up, she was the one I wanted to be. Had some success in that."

"I do think though that we should give him one more question before I explain things. Joseph- Joey. One last question?"

"Okay. Two parts though. First, where am I? Second part: When do I get untied and out of here?"

"You get loose from that bed when we have finished a successful conversation. I decide successful. As to when you leave, you don't. At least in body. Never. Where are you? This place is where you're safe. We call it Sanctuary."

Joey: More Sanctuary

Theme: *Joey (from A Small death)* Samantha Crain;

Storm paused for a long moment. Then went on.

"Your out-of-body travels are done now. We keep the bodies here in a kind of permanent coma. Safe and, barring catastrophe, we are always here."

I interrupted: *"Always is a long time! What if something kills all of you?"*

Storm laughed. Said *"That seems to me would be catastrophic!"*

And then: *"But it's my turn to talk now. Time for you to listen."*

I shut up. For now.

"We keep track of these OBE Ghost Walkers. Especially the dangerous prisoners. You see, we can do that too. We rein the ghost walking of our guests in. We have their sedated bodies and, without them, the connection is broken and true death occurs. We just keep everybody safe, visitors and visited."

I opened my mouth with questions. Thought better of it.

She nodded approval and continued.

"Roger is the main doctor at your prison. He drugged you with something to lower your pulse and respiration to an undetectable level. Get used to it. He declared you as deceased and claimed you then were cremated. Sand in a funeral jar to relatives. Real body here. Standard procedure. You're different though. Not really a menace if you can avoid it. Much more interesting though, you are permanently connected to your son. By now, a part of who he is, even as a grown man. We will not interfere with that since it seems to be motivated by love. So even as your body remains here, you may still experience life outside as part of him. And, hopefully, will not interfere since he is by now his own person. Maybe some advice if he asks for it? IF."

This was a lot to think about. Even so, I nodded yes. She smiled.

"*Seems that you can understand now, Joey. Except for Roger here and a few others, we are all ghost walkers here. Our bodies resting quietly, never aging. So. If you understand, you can get up now and join us to watch a sunrise. You'll know if your boy needs you. Rise up!*"

Now how in hell can I do that? Still strapped in to that hospital bed. Noticing IV and leads into my body.

Maybe I can test this challenge with one hand. I tried to raise my right.

It came through the ties, floated right through!

In a few minutes I was standing free. Still felt the connection, lifeline really, to the body, now sleeping again. And aware that my son was aware that my presence continued with him.

Okay! Where are we anyway? Outside I mean.

Let's see that sunrise.

Leonard: Ghost Visit

Theme: *Spirit in the Sky* Norman Greenbaum; *Summertime* Audra McDonald; *I Feel Like Singing* Dan Hicks

Summer. Though for me, feels like autumn edging to winter.

Time has passed. Aunt Rhoda and Uncle Manny are not so young any more.

But the two adult daughters they birthed and raised, my wonderful cousins, stand by them. A great family.

I'm there when I can be too.

Just me though now in my home, more than enough.

My only regret is the loss of my father.

No longer in my head, no matter how I call him.

Officially died in jail, no funeral. I suppose.

If ghosts are real, some nights I invite him to visit.

No luck.

Sometimes in earlier years he studied OBE (out-of-body) and even sometimes appeared faintly as he mastered it. But nothing now.

Then, in the middle of one night, he appeared. Not faint, vivid! And looking really happy! The other ghost with him was a beautiful woman, as large as him.

Asked for a ghost and got two!

Wrong. They, in OBE form, claimed to be alive. More! They invited me to their hidden home, address supplied, day of arrival included.

And then gone.

To see my father, now separate but alive! I made arrangements to disappear myself.

Storm: Time Travel for my Uncle

Theme: *Sweet Dreams* Annie Lennox; *Time will Tell* Susan Anton (*Wizards* theme).

I loved meeting Joey's son, even if by hazy OBE.

Back in my body, got me thinking of my own family.

Our family name actually was "Storm" although a German root was "Sturm" for generations lost in antiquity. But with a last name like that, growing up as "Storm" hit like a guided missile.

Then I sat quietly, alone, remembering my Uncle Joseph. How wonderful he was to me growing up. Full of stories and treats, genuine affection (rare in my family). He loved children.

Too much.

He led boy's camps and outings in the summer, worked at a local school the rest of the year. Most of the boys liked him though some found him *too* nice. Uncomfortable.

Joseph was very careful to not let his attraction to these boys lead to anything wrong.

He was protective of their childhood. But his dreams at night were not so circumspect. They were romantic, erotic, disturbing.

He knew that in his time people who felt like him were considered pariahs. Perverted, predatory, diagnosed as a disease. Sure he had read of ancient cultures like Greece and Rome, or even in some tribal nations, his attractions were unremarkable. Not where he lived. Not when he lived.

Joseph confided his fears to a young man who he had known for years, trusted. The young man kept his secrets as promised. Except, as a good Catholic, in confession.

Confession is also protected for secrets. But there is a loophole. The priest who took his confession related it in the sanctity of his own confession. That soon made its way to the Bishop, still in confidence of course.

The Bishop, well aware of some of his own predatory priests, considered that some publicity diverting attention from the church could be helpful. Joseph wasn't Catholic.

The school fired Joseph. He was publicly shunned.

Feeling overwhelmed. He killed himself.

I was devastated. Gradually learned the why and the how. But too late.

If I could only talk to him then as the person I am now, I might save this wonderful spirit, my dear uncle Joseph.

I confided this to Joey. I've always had to rise to Joey's high opinion of me.

He just said *"Then find a way to go back in time and then talk to him."*

Sure. I had no time machine. Wish I did. So I just slept on it.

Woke up with an idea.

If my body was not rooted always is space, we do go out of body a lot now, what about time?

At first no luck with OBE time travel, not even by a second.

Then I realized that I did have a temporal road to my past. Myself!

Every time I remembered an earlier event in my life, I was connecting to my own past.

Not literally of course. Though parapsychologist William Braud had written that effective therapy with an adult can remove trauma from the child that became that adult- can ripple back in time. (William did not speculate about the adult having trauma rippling this to herself as a child. Eduardo Duran took this forward in time showing intergenerational trauma rippling to descendants. I love reading this stuff!)

Now once I learned hypnosis, I liked to go back to key events in my life, nice ones like a sixth birthday, and look through my young eyes at myself in the mirror that day. Of course I thought of these as just memories. Still, when I look in the mirror now, I wonder if an older me is looking back.

Well, what if I go back to my younger self the summer when my uncle was considering suicide? Would my younger self let me in? Just for a little talk?

Joey had done this in his own life already. He had thought to go back and redo the trauma of his wife's death and the rest. But that overwhelming trauma had blocked him from reaching his younger self.

He had resolved the trauma in himself through auto-hypnosis. Relived it all again and again from a distance. Until it no longer was trauma for the older safer Joey though it still was a deep sense of loss that seemed endless.

He sent a Latin curse through time to those doing that whole bloody disaster: *Pox Vobiscom*. Felt a little better.

Then he realized that if he had succeeded he would have changed the future from that day, probably erasing his unique connection to his son, accomplishing who he had become, and never being with me.

So he stopped trying. Warned me to be careful.

But that aside, Joey was encouraging.

I agreed to try. Just to comfort Joseph.

Worked!

The night was late but Joseph answered his door. Let me in.

Leonard: Reunion

Themes: *Reunion* Bobbie Gentry; *Sing Our Song* Buffy Saint-Marie; *Up Where We Belong* Buffy Saint-Marie/Joe Cocker & Jennifer Warnes

> *"This is a new day, fresh, untouched. What will you do with it?"*
>
> -Native American Church

Storm sat facing us. We sat alone together around a small circular table.

Joey looked like he felt how I did, feelings I easily receive from him, even now.

An immense relief. Family. Freedom. Finally.

Plus love for Storm, above and beyond this miracle. Reciprocated.

In a dimly lit room, no windows, no apparent light source. Private. Happy.

I'm finally with my living father. No need for mind whispers any more.

Feelings swamped them. Joy. Satisfaction. We had made it.

Joey looked like he felt all that too. Feelings from him that I still receive even now. An immense relief. Family. Freedom. Finally.

Plus love for Storm, above and beyond this miracle. Reciprocated.

Storm told us both to relax as she had a fresh experience to celebrate this reunion.

She hung onto our hands as the lighting faded to total dark.

A sense of external warmth blankets us. Something mixing love and joy. My father and me, now connected in the dark by the soft hands of a woman.

Not Storm sitting opposite us, holding our other hands. These new hands radiating reassurance, pleasure, delight.

We all swam with the experience.

Such things were to be expected from Storm yet for me, this was almost overwhelming.

In minutes or more, time estimation impossible, our hands were freed, soft lights back, all three of us catching our breath.

Joey broke the silence.

"Whatever that was, it was magnificent. Thank you."

I agreed. Knew not to ask questions. But waited for answers. Maybe.

Food was brought in. A small beautiful meal.

Some quiet conversation. So much time ahead now for Joey and me to catch up.

Though Joey had missed very little of my life to that point.

We three shared stories.

Storm's are the most interesting, most unknown until now. She seemed to be aware of our more recent lives quite well. Hers were amazing.

Eventually we began to tire. Time for good nights and thanks.

I thanked Storm for bringing my father back after his "death" so we could finally share a family future.

I thanked her for now being with my father and me.

Joey did the same, added how he wished my birth mother could see how I had survived, thrived, turned out, and how happy he finally was being with Storm and me.

Still, he added that Storm's power to bring him back from his prison death did not extend to the true death waiting for us all.

What she had done was more than wonderful enough.

Actual death and what might follow remained a mystery to him, beyond reach, beyond the powers of any of us. Including Storm.

A somber moment.

Storm had an intense smile. Seemed unwelcome to hear family think that her powers had limits.

She spoke with quiet strength now: *"Joey. I think you're missing the point about that mystery being out of reach. About what you already experienced tonight."*

Joey louder now: *"Trina? Leonard's mother?"*

Storm with a voice echoing from all the room's walls: *"I found her!"*

He Died for This Dream

Themes: *Greensleeves; Amazing Grace* Soweto Gospel Choir

Greensleeves is at least 700 years old and, as such, may be the oldest music to be found today in Western culture.

Royalties no longer apply.

Of much more historical value is s time statue from August 28th 1963 when Reverend Dr. Martin Luther King Jr. shared his dream with 250,000 civil rights supporters from the steps of the Lincoln Memorial in Washington, D.C. Plus millions more seeing it on television all across the globe then and as continually replayed in the years since.

His dream was a gift to the human family, defining a best future, clarifying a direction to march for, and one he strove to actualize for the following years.

Yet there were just five more years before he was killed, never to reach the age of 40.

His gift remains. Providing hope and direction, against the growing challenges of today.

Especially today. An essential path.

I will share his speech as a final dream in this book.

Not now his or mine, but ours.

First though I thank Dr. Robert Lee Green for those times he brought me with him to his support of Dr. King and his movement, between the years of his shared dream speech and the final year when he died for it.

Here is his dream.

August 28th 1963

"I am happy to join with you today in what will go down in history as the greatest demonstration for freedom in the history of our nation.

Five score years ago, a great American, in whose symbolic shadow we stand today, signed the Emancipation Proclamation. This momentous decree came as a great beacon light of hope to millions of Negro slaves who had been seared in the flames of withering injustice. It came as a joyous daybreak to end the long night of their captivity.

But one hundred years later, the Negro still is not free. One hundred years later, the life of the Negro is still sadly crippled by the manacles of segregation and the chains of discrimination. One hundred years later, the Negro lives on a lonely island of poverty in the midst of a vast ocean of material prosperity. One hundred years later, the Negro is still languishing in the corners of American society and finds himself an exile in his own land. So we have come here today to dramatize a shameful condition.

In a sense we have come to our nation's capital to cash a check. When the architects of our republic wrote the magnificent words of the Constitution and the Declaration of Independence, they were signing a promissory note to which every American was to fall heir. This note was a promise that all men, yes, black men as well as white men, would be guaranteed the unalienable rights of life, liberty, and the pursuit of happiness.

It is obvious today that America has defaulted on this promissory note insofar as her citizens of color are concerned. Instead of honoring this sacred obligation, America has given the Negro people a bad check, a check which has come back marked "insufficient funds." But we refuse to believe that the bank of justice is bankrupt. We refuse to believe that there are insufficient funds in the great vaults of opportunity of this nation. So we have come to cash this check — a check that will give us upon demand the riches of freedom and the security of justice. We have also come to this hallowed spot to remind America of the fierce urgency of now. This is no time to engage in the luxury of cooling off or to take the tranquilizing drug of gradualism. Now is the time to make real the promises of democracy. Now is the time to rise from the dark and desolate valley of segregation to the sunlit path of racial justice. Now is the time to lift our nation from the quick sands of racial injustice to the solid rock of brotherhood. Now is the time to make justice a reality for all of God's children.

It would be fatal for the nation to overlook the urgency of the moment. This sweltering summer of the Negro's legitimate discontent will not pass until there is an invigorating autumn of freedom and equality. Nineteen sixty-three is not an end, but a beginning. Those who hope that the Negro needed to blow off steam and will now be content will have a rude awakening if the nation returns to business as usual. There will be neither rest nor tranquility in America until the Negro is granted his citizenship rights. The whirlwinds of revolt will continue to shake the foundations of our nation until the bright day of justice emerges.

But there is something that I must say to my people who stand on the warm threshold which leads into the palace of justice. In the process of gaining our rightful place we must not be guilty of wrongful deeds. Let us not seek to satisfy our thirst for freedom by drinking from the cup of bitterness and hatred.

We must forever conduct our struggle on the high plane of dignity and discipline. We must not allow our creative protest to degenerate into physical violence. Again and again we must rise to the majestic heights of meeting physical force with soul force. The marvelous new militancy which has engulfed the Negro community must not lead us to a distrust of all white people, for many of our white brothers, as evidenced by their presence here today, have come to realize that their destiny is tied up with our destiny. They have come to realize that their freedom is inextricably bound to our freedom. We cannot walk alone.

As we walk, we must make the pledge that we shall always march ahead. We cannot turn back. There are those who are asking the devotees of civil rights, "When will you be satisfied?" We can never be satisfied as long as the Negro is the victim of the unspeakable horrors of police brutality. We can never be satisfied, as long as our bodies, heavy with the fatigue of travel, cannot gain lodging in the motels of the highways and the hotels of the cities. We cannot be satisfied as long as the Negro's basic mobility is from a smaller ghetto to a larger one. We can never be satisfied as long as our children are stripped of their selfhood and robbed of their dignity by signs stating "For Whites Only". We cannot be satisfied as long as a Negro in Mississippi cannot vote and a Negro in New York believes he has nothing for which to vote. No, no, we are not satisfied, and we will not be satisfied until justice rolls down like waters and righteousness like a mighty stream.

I am not unmindful that some of you have come here out of great trials and tribulations. Some of you have come fresh from narrow jail cells. Some of you have come from areas where your quest for freedom left you battered by the storms of persecution and staggered by the winds of police brutality. You have been the veterans of creative suffering. Continue to work with the faith that unearned suffering is redemptive.

Go back to Mississippi, go back to Alabama, go back to South Carolina, go back to Georgia, go back to Louisiana, go back to the slums and ghettos of our northern cities, knowing that somehow this situation can and will be changed. Let us not wallow in the valley of despair.

I say to you today, my friends, so even though we face the difficulties of today and tomorrow, I still have a dream. It is a dream deeply rooted in the American dream.

I have a dream that one day this nation will rise up and live out the true meaning of its creed: "We hold these truths to be self-evident: that all men are created equal."

I have a dream that one day on the red hills of Georgia the sons of former slaves and the sons of former slave owners will be able to sit down together at the table of brotherhood.

I have a dream that one day even the state of Mississippi, a state sweltering with the heat of injustice, sweltering with the heat of oppression, will be transformed into an oasis of freedom and justice.

I have a dream that my four little children will one day live in a nation where they will not be judged by the color of their skin but by the content of their character.

I have a dream today.

I have a dream that one day, down in Alabama, with its vicious racists, with its governor having his lips dripping with the words of interposition and nullification; one day right there in Alabama, little black boys and black girls will be able to join hands with little white boys and white girls as sisters and brothers.

I have a dream today.

I have a dream that one day every valley shall be exalted, every hill and mountain shall be made low, the rough places will be made plain, and the crooked places will be made straight, and the glory of the Lord shall be revealed, and all flesh shall see it together.

DREAMS AND TIME STATUES

This is our hope. This is the faith that I go back to the South with. With this faith we will be able to hew out of the mountain of despair a stone of hope. With this faith we will be able to transform the jangling discords of our nation into a beautiful symphony of brotherhood. With this faith we will be able to work together, to pray together, to struggle together, to go to jail together, to stand up for freedom together, knowing that we will be free one day.

This will be the day when all of God's children will be able to sing with a new meaning, "My country, 'tis of thee, sweet land of liberty, of thee I sing. Land where my fathers died, land of the pilgrim's pride, from every mountainside, let freedom ring."

And if America is to be a great nation this must become true. So let freedom ring from the prodigious hilltops of New Hampshire. Let freedom ring from the mighty mountains of New York. Let freedom ring from the heightening Alleghenies of Pennsylvania!

Let freedom ring from the snowcapped Rockies of Colorado!

Let freedom ring from the curvaceous slopes of California!

But not only that; let freedom ring from Stone Mountain of Georgia!

Let freedom ring from Lookout Mountain of Tennessee!

Let freedom ring from every hill and molehill of Mississippi. From every mountainside, let freedom ring.

And when this happens, when we allow freedom to ring, when we let it ring from every village and every hamlet, from every state and every city, we will be able to speed up that day when all of God's children, black men and white men, Jews and Gentiles, Protestants and Catholics, will be able to join hands and sing in the words of the old Negro spiritual, "Free at last! Free at last! Thank God Almighty, we are free at last!"

Closing theme now: *Amazing Grace* Soweto Gospel Choir

After: Jake Explains Time

Theme: *Great Grandfather* Bo Diddley

1957. Jakob von Uexkull first made me more fully aware of the varying perceptual time world of animals:

"Karl Ernst von Baer has made it clear that time is the product of a subject. Time as a succession of moments varies from one Umwelt to another, according to the number of moments experienced by different subjects within the same span of time. A moment is the smallest indivisible time vessel, for it is the expressions of an indivisible elementary sensation, the so-called moment sign. As already stated, the duration of a human moment amounts to 1/18 of a second. Furthermore, the moment is identical for all sense modalities, since all sensations are accompanied by the same moment sign.

The human ear does not discriminate eighteen air vibrations in one second, but hears them as one sound. It has been found that eighteen taps applied to the skin within one second are felt as even pressure.

Cinematography projects environmental motions onto a screen at their accustomed tempo. The single pictures then follow each other in tiny jerks of 1/18 second.

If we wish to observe motions too swift for the human eye, we resort to slow-motion photography. This is a technique by which more than eighteen pictures are taken per second, and then projected at a normal tempo. Motor processes are thus extended over a longer span of time, and processes too swift for our human time-tempo (of 18 per second), such as the wing beat of birds and insects, can be made visible. As slow motion-motion photography slows motor processes down, the time contractor speeds them up. If a process is photographed once an hour and then presented at the rate of 1/18 second, it is condensed into a short space of time. In this way, processes too slow for our human tempo, such as the blossoming of a flower, can be brought within the range of our perception.

The question arises whether there are animals whose perceptual time consists of shorter or longer moments than ours, and in whose Umwelt motor processes are consequently enacted more slowly or more quickly than in ours.

The first experiments of this kind were made by a young German scientist. Later, with the collaboration of another, he studied especially the reaction of the fighting fish to its own mirror image. The fighting fish does not recognize its own reflection if is shown him eighteen times per second. It must be presented to the fighting fish at least thirty times per second. A third student trained the fighting fish to snap toward their food if a gray disc was rotated behind it. On the other hand, if a disc with black and white sectors was turned slowly, it acted as a "warning sign," for in this case the fish received a light shock when they approached their food. After this training, if the rotation speed of the black and white disc was gradually increased, the avoiding reactions became more uncertain at a certain speed, and soon thereafter they shifted to the opposite. This did not happen until the black sectors followed each other within 1/50 second. At this speed the black and white signal had become gray. This proves conclusively that in the world of these fish, who feed on fast moving prey, all motor processes – as in the case of slow-motion photography – appear at reduced speed.

A vineyard snail is placed on a rubber ball which, carried by water, slides under it without friction. The snail's shell is held in place by a bracket. Thus the snail, unhampered by its crawling movements, remains in the same place. If a small stick is then moved up to its foot, the snail will climb up on it. If the snail is given one to three taps with the stick each second, it will turn away, but if four or more taps are administered per second, it will begin to climb onto the stick. In the snail's world a rod that oscillates four times per second has become stationary. We may infer from this that the snail's receptor time moves at a tempo of three to four moments per second. As a result, all motor processes in the snail's world occur much faster than in ours. Nor do its own motions seem slower to the snail than ours do to us."

(von Uexkull 1957)

Learning to perceive the *Umwelt* (world view) of animals has the added benefit of enhancing empathy for our own species.

Acknowledgements

Theme: *If I Didn't Care* Inkspots

This 2024 book in the *Time Statues* series has mostly new material. A few portions from my earlier books have been modified, or excerpted here where it fits. With author permission.

Thanks again first to Asya Blue whose artistry and skills recently completed the 2023 five book *Time Statues Revisited* series, and then the final 2023 *Future Time Statues* one. Now, with the next two 2024 books, the final ones in the series, *Time Statue Dreams* and *Time Statues Harvest,* she and her staff have continued their essential contributions.

Becky Owl Morgan's carefully thorough editing and counsel was again essential for everything written here. And ongoing encouragement from Tom Hanrahan, Mindy Caruso, Ron Slosky, Angela and Conrad Laran, Stan Krippner, Ann and Ken Yabusaki, and of course Angel Kwanyin Morgan.

Otherwise, pretty much the same as in earlier *Time Statues* work: I thank my past editors from different printing opportunities who encouraged me to write whatever I chose, even if without statistics, graphs, tables, footnotes, or scientific jargon. I was told to just call it *"Commentary"*. Or just write it.

In this I think of Valerie Hearn, with the staff at the *Cambridge University Press*, and Valentine McKay-Riddell, with her staff at the

Four Winds Journal and the *Winds of Change Press*. After decades of publishing about a hundred scientific journal articles and 14 earlier books, it felt good to write the seven time statues books freely and outside the confines of professional custom. I thank colleague Charles Tart who shared his own writing strategy: '*Just write what you really want to say. Then, as needed, you can add any citations, references, footnotes, and anything else an editor suggests.*'

Original material in this series is supplemented with my excerpts and illustrations from the *Four Winds Journal*, the Cambridge University Press *Journal of Tropical Psychology*, the *Bulletin of the International Association of Applied Psychology*: Supplement to *Applied Psychology: an International Review, Trauma Psychology in Context: International Vignettes and Applications from a Lifespan Clinical-Community Psychology Perspective, Opportunity's Shadow and the Bee Moth Effect: When Danger Transforms Community, Unfortunate Baby Names,* and the journal *International Psychology.*

As to the key mission of understanding the strange world we live in, and what we can do about it, I thank my Guides. Those include Robert Lee Green, Martin Luther King Jr., David Cheek, Michael Knowles, Rollo May, Nathan Hare, Fred Luskin, Sidney Farber, Robert Dattila, or mentors like Stanley Ratner, Bert Karon, Hans Toch, Lois Fisher, Helga Doblin, Cinnamon Morgan, Canadian-born Angel Morgan, plus the multitudes of my friends, teachers, parents and other relatives (my brother Nelson Morgan and forever sister Pat Norman come to mind, as do her children Elise, James, plus certainly Angela and her husband Conrad Laran). Also Michael Butz, Ben Tong, Ron Slosky, Len Elkind, Ann Yabusaki, and the other thousands of once students in six+ decades of teaching who have taught me much in return.

I have special new appreciation for brilliant editor/inspiration Becky Owl Morgan, Mikael David Owl, guest contributor Angel Morgan, and the relentless motivating encouragement of Dr. Carl Word, Tom Hanrahan, Dorinda Fox, and Dr. Robert Lee Green. Dr. Roland Garcia impressively provided key focused feedback early on for a much improved reorganization. And the example set by my once long lost cousin, the illustrious award winning author Tom Farber.

Respect is due the earlier *Time Statues* reviewers that mixed insight and comment with their own encouragement: Lois Bridges, Valentine McKay Riddell, Theodore Ransaw, Charles Tart, Hans Toch, Ann Yabusaki, with again Nelson Morgan and Robert Lee Green. Great thanks also to Ben Tong for his many contributing illustrations and insightful historical context.

As ever, a thankful appreciation for our recently departed friend Dr. Nathan Hare. He was the founder of university Ethnic Studies in an era *then* while continuation of his contribution is needed *next* more than ever *now*.

Finally, in continuing memory of Ben Camo, our granddaughter Ava's father:

Octogenarian memory can be tricky. You may be curious about anybody deserving to be acknowledged here that I inadvertently left out. Hope not. But an option we can always use is the answers source we learn about all day long on TV commercials.

Ask your doctor.

DREAMS AND TIME STATUES

"When you sit with a nice girl for two hours, you think it's only a minute. But when you sit on a hot stove for a minute, you think its two hours. That's relativity."
(Albert Einstein, 1954)

Author

Theme: *Time Will Tell (movie theme from The Wizards)* Susan Anton

Born in the lull between the two world wars, he shares his lifespan perspectives on today's interesting times.

Robert F. Morgan, Ph.D. is a Life Member of the American Psychological Association. An NIMH Pre-Doctoral Fellow at Michigan State University, he continued with more than 50 years of post-doctoral practice and teaching experience.

A former speech collaborator and project consultant for organizations including Dr. Martin Luther King Jr.'s SCLC, he was founding editor of the Cambridge University Press *Journal of Tropical Psychology*, and founder of the Division of Applied Gerontology in the International Association of Applied Psychology (IAAP).

He has overseen 126 psychology doctoral dissertations in California, Singapore, and Australia, along with a contemporary trauma psychology seminar at the University of New Mexico.

He has published more than a hundred articles and 25 books on topics including life span psychology, trauma psychology in context, applied gerontology, international psychology, and even unfortunate baby names.

Only semi-retired, he avoids a lethargic status by continuing to think and write. He also hopes to avoid Lincoln's prescient warning: *"It is better to be silent and thought a fool than to open one's mouth and remove all doubt."* Well, his readers will continue to be the judge of that.

Books by Robert F. Morgan

Time Statue Harvest from the 21st Century
Time Statue Harvest from the 20th Century
Time Statue Dreams
Time Statues Revisited: Book One: On the Job.
  Book Two: Language & Influence
  Book Three: Citizenship
  Book Four: Non-Human Relatives
 Book Five: Human Family
Time Statues
Trauma Psychology in Context: International Vignettes and Applications
Opportunity's Shadow & the Bee Moth Effect: When Danger Transforms Community
Growing Younger: How to Measure & Change Body Age
The Iatrogenics Handbook: Research & Practice in Helping Professions
Training the Time Sense: Hypnotic & Conditioning Approaches
Unfortunate baby names: Slattery's complete collection with the most notable thousands for dramatic and other usage
Electroshock: the Case Against.
Directory of International Consultants in Psychology
Interventions in Applied Gerontology
Measurement of Human Aging in Applied Gerontology
Should the Insanity Defense be Abolished?
Conquest of Aging: Modern Measurement & Intervention
The Effective Verbal Adaptation (EVA) test: Parts A & B
The Educational Status of Children in a District without Public Schools: CRP 3221.
The Educational Status of Children during the First Year Following Four Years of Little or No Schooling: CRP 2498.
Uncas Slattery and the Muddy Chuckle

www.ingramcontent.com/pod-product-compliance
Lightning Source LLC
Chambersburg PA
CBHW041135110526
44590CB00027B/4025